## Praise for *SEE HOW SHE RUNS*

"A wonderful, insightful story of the making of a superstar by one of America's very best sportswriters."—David Halberstam

"A fascinating look at Marion Jones."—*Publishers Weekly*

"A wonderful book, etched from the headlines that have made Marion Jones a household name in the world of sports."—*Track and Field News*

"There is so much to like about Marion Jones. There is so much to like about *See How She Runs*."—Harvey Frommer, *SportwritersDirect*

"An excellent new biography of Marion Jones."—*London Telegraph*

"An empowering biography of the woman called the next great sports superstar. Marion Jones is the fastest woman alive and Rapoport's remarkable profile of this great athlete lays the cornerstone to what promises to be a stunning career."—*Black Issues Book Review*

"An awesome biography . . . all the scoop on the fastest woman in the world can be found somewhere in these pages."—*Teen People Book Club*

"An invaluable, inspirational, contemporary biography of a positive role model."—*School Library Journal*

# SEE HOW SHE RUNS

1985

Hi my name is Marion Jones. I'm 5 feet 2 inches. I am 10 years old and in the sixth grade. I think I have a nice personality. I have a pretty good grades and my weight is 85 pounds.

My hobbies are running and gymnastics. I like running because I can beat almost everyone at my school. I like gymnastics because I can do all sort of tricks and I'm very flexible in some ways.

My plans for the future are to be in the 1992 olympics. I've been training a lot, and the boys at my school are good practice. I know if I don't get in the olympics I have to have a backup so I plan to be electrical engineer like my uncle.

# SEE HOW SHE RUNS

# *Marion Jones*

## & THE MAKING OF A CHAMPION

by Ron Rapoport

 Amistad *An Imprint of HarperCollinsPublishers*

HarperCollins books may be purchased for educational, business, or sales promotional use. For information, please write: Special Markets Department, HarperCollins Publishers Inc., 10 East 53rd Street, New York, NY 10022.

Originally published in hardcover in a different form in 2000 by Algonquin Books of Chapel Hill.

Grateful acknowledgment for the use of photographs is made to the following:
pp. iv, xviii–1: Courtesy Marion Jones; p. 79: *All photos,* Courtesy Marion Jones; p. 80: *Top right,* ©1991 DUOMO/Paul J. Sutton. *Bottom right,* ©Photo Run. *Top left and bottom left,* Courtesy Marion Jones; p. 81: ©The Herald-Sun/BillWillcox; p. 82: *Top right and bottom right,* Courtesy Marion Jones. *Top left,* ©The Herald-Sun/Bill Willcox. *Bottom left,* Courtesy Marion Jones; p. 83: *Top and bottom,* ©Photo Run; p. 84: *Top right,* ©1998 DUOMO/Paul J. Sutton. *Middle right,* Courtesy Marion Jones. *Top left and bottom,* ©Photo Run; pp. 124–125: ©1999 DUOMO/Steven E. Sutton; p. 145: *Top right,* ©1999 DUOMO/Paul J. Sutton. *Middle right,* Courtesy Marion Jones. *Bottom,* ©1999 DUOMO/Paul J. Sutton. *Top left,* ©1999 DUOMO/Steven E. Sutton; p. 146: *Top right,* © 1999 DUOMO/Paul J. Sutton. *Bottom right,* ©Photo Run. *Top left and bottom left,* Courtesy Marion Jones; p. 147: *Top right,* ©DeFrisco 1999. *Bottom right,* ©1999 DUOMO/Paul J. Sutton. *Top and bottom left,* ©Photo Run; p. 148: *Top,* ©1999 DUOMO/Chris Cole. *Bottom,* ©1999 DUOMO/Paul J. Sutton; pp. 208–209: Bill Frakes/David Callow/Sports Illustrated.

FIRST AMISTAD EDITION 2001.

*Designed by Anne Winslow*

Printed on acid-free paper

Library of Congress Cataloging-in-Publication Data is available upon request.

ISBN 0-06-093592-8

02   03   04   05   RRD   10   9   8   7   6   5   4   3   2

For Marion and C. J.

*Champions in anybody's book*

_____

# CONTENTS

# INTRODUCTION

When I first started working on this book, I felt as if I had known Marion almost half my life. Then I realized it was almost half of hers.

As a sports columnist for a Los Angeles newspaper located one valley inland from Marion's home in Ventura County in the early 1990s, I soon discovered there were only two high school sports seasons in our area: football and Marion Jones.

California is not a state easily impressed by high school phenoms. With its large population, its endless summers, and its tradition of physical education, it has long been a training ground for a procession of professional and Olympic athletes.

But even in this seen-it-all environment, Marion's exploits were special. California interscholastic sports officials still argue over which was her greater accomplishment: beating so many older and more mature girls to win the state 100- and 200-meter dash championships as a freshman, or winning those events in the next three years and, as a senior, adding a ninth title in the long jump as well. Marion's basketball talents were equally prodigious, so perhaps it's easy to understand why those who follow high school sports in California still speak of her in hushed tones.

Marion's departure for the University of North Carolina was no handicap to those of us curious to see what would happen next. Soon after she arrived on campus, she was appointed playmaker and leader of the basketball team, which responded by winning the NCAA championship her freshman year.

The following season, North Carolina played in a postseason tournament at UCLA and I made it a point to be a part of the press contingent there to write the inevitable local-girl-makes-good-and-returns-home stories. Although I felt as if we were old friends by then, and although I had met Marion briefly on a magazine assignment in Chapel Hill several months earlier, I realized this was the first time I would have an actual conversation with her.

I can remember almost nothing about what we talked about that day—probably her team's chances against Stanford and how much she was looking forward to playing in front of her family and friends—but I cannot forget my astonishment while the interviews were taking place. Never before had I met a young athlete with such poise, charm, and intelligence, or one with such a sense of delight. I hadn't met many older ones, either.

Marion knew where the cameras were—the photographers couldn't get enough of her smile—and which direction the questions were coming from, too. She controlled the interview session like a veteran politician, saying exactly what she wanted without giving any indication that her answers were calculated, and never letting us forget that she was, after all, only nineteen years old.

How did she do that? I wondered as I walked off the court. Can such a weighty word as *charisma* possibly be applied to someone so young? The question was answered when that word cropped up again and again in my conversations with the people who know Marion best.

There were other forces she could not control, however, and, as they tugged at her for the next two years, I lost track of Marion.

There were two serious injuries, a difficult career choice that left hurt feelings behind at her alma mater, and troublesome family matters to deal with. During Marion's junior year in college, she was unable to compete at all, an agonizing thing to someone for whom sports had always been both a joy and a refuge.

And then one day, she was back. Back with the kind of authority few athletes have ever enjoyed. After what amounted to a four-year absence from track and field, and after only a few months of serious training, she won the 1997 U.S. championship in the 100-meter dash and the long jump at Indianapolis. Several months later, in Athens, she won the world championship in the 100 meters and became the fastest woman in the world.

But just as the international track and field community was recovering from that shock, Marion took it one step further the next season. Participating in a world tour that was unprecedented both for its ambition and the eyebrows it raised among the experts, Marion entered meets at a frenzied pace all over the world, returning home just long enough to become the first woman in fifty years to win three titles at the U.S. championships in New Orleans. In all, she took part in thirty-seven different competitions in 1998. She won thirty-six of them. By the time the year was over, Marion was number one in the world in the 100, the 200, and the long jump, and she was knocking on the door of three world records.

In a sense, she had returned full circle. Just as the argument about her high school accomplishments continues, so does the debate over whether her return in 1997 was a greater feat than her triumphant world tour the following year. This was a debate, it seems reasonable to note, about a woman who had yet to celebrate her twenty-third birthday.

Late in 1998, when Marion announced she planned to add two relays to her repertoire at the 2000 Olympics and try for an unprecedented five gold medals, I was hooked. The Games in Sydney were still almost two years away, enough time to satisfy my curiosity about Marion, and perhaps that of a broader audience as well. It would be a pity, I thought, if we only came to know her during the Olympics for her accomplishments on the track and not for the story that lay behind them, and for those personal qualities I had glimpsed that day at UCLA.

WHEN I ASKED MARION if she would help me write a book about her, she quickly agreed, with the understanding that the manuscript would be hers to review. Though she was competing in her critically important pre-Olympic year, she threw herself into the project with the same sense of purpose she applies to everything else.

She drew me into her circle, put me in touch with her family, friends, former coaches and teammates, and spoke into my tape recorder at such length that finally, on a rainy day at the North Carolina State University track in Raleigh, we looked at each other and laughed. I had no more questions and she had no more answers.

I also accompanied Marion to a number of U.S. track meets in 1999, and to the World Championships in Seville, where she provided me with an access that proved crucial to my understanding of a world-champion athlete's competitive life. At her meets and practice sessions, Marion and the people around her reacted with good-natured tolerance to the presence of a stranger eavesdropping on their conversations and standing around waiting to see what they would do next.

"We've had some people asking who you are," Marion's manager, Charlie Wells, said one day after I had accompanied the group onto a practice track before a meet. "We told them you're security."

SEVERAL MONTHS PRIOR to the Olympics, before the first edition of this book was published, Marion and I were back at work on an expanded version to include her 2000 season that would culminate in Sydney. Since we were dealing with a period of only a few months, I assumed we would need one relatively short chapter to bring her story up to date through the Games.

But in July, as I was standing near the long-jump pit at the U.S. Olympic Trials in Sacramento, I began to realize it wasn't going to be that simple. My notebook was already jammed with the details of Marion's comeback from the career-threatening injury that ended her 1999 season prematurely. The Olympic Trials themselves were proving to be exciting beyond compare. And now, after two fouls, here she was, down to one last jump that would determine whether she would even be *allowed* to compete for five gold medals in Sydney.

She certainly hadn't made it easy on herself, I told her after she made her qualifying distance with room to spare.

"Is it ever easy?" she said with a grin. It was a remark that would prove, before the summer was out, more prophetic than either of us could have imagined.

In the two months between the Olympic Trials and the Games themselves, Marion was everywhere. Virtually every television show discussing the Olympics focused on her. Newspaper special sections devoted lengthy articles to her. Annie Leibovitz shot her for the cover of *Women's Sports & Fitness. Sports Illustrated for Women* and *Sports Illustrated for Kids* made her their Olympic cover girl. *Scientific American* drew a robotic diagram over her picture for the cover of a special issue devoted to "Building the Elite Athlete." And the week before the Olympics, as if to confirm she was at that moment the biggest story in the world, Marion appeared on the cover of both *Time* and *Newsweek.*

Then she went to Sydney, where her Olympic experience became at once a lifelong dream come true and a week-long nightmare.

As I watched her deal with the enormous pressure she was under—some of which she had been able to prepare for and some that struck from out of the blue—two thoughts occurred to me. The first was that the firestorm of controversy that engulfed her in Sydney could be understood only if it was described within the context of international Olympic politics. The second was that despite Marion's many great performances in the past, both on and off the track, this was her finest hour.

Marion didn't flinch from her end of the bargain—she told me everything she was thinking and of her wildly fluctuating emotions during those tumultuous days—and I was determined to tell the story as fully and accurately as possible. For all these reasons, this book has grown by nearly a third since it was first published. Those who read the earlier version will, I hope, want to know what happened during the year Marion overcame so many obstacles to become one of the greatest stars in Olympic history. New readers, of course, can now learn about the woman who climbed to the podium in Sydney time after time to have yet another medal hung around her neck.

Two years ago, I began this book in the belief that Marion

might well be the world's greatest athlete. I finished it thinking she is also one of its most remarkable young women. Here, then, is her story. So far.

Ron Rapoport
Chicago, Illinois
December 2000

# SEE HOW SHE RUNS

**Part 1**

*Beginnings*

# 1

*I*n 1983, when Marion Jones was eight years old and had graduated from T-ball to Little League, she found herself not only competing against boys, but beating them. Once, with a runner on second base, Marion hit the ball beyond the outfielders and, pigtails flying, raced around the bases so quickly she overtook the boy ahead of her by the time he had reached third.

"Don't pass him!" her mother called from the stands, and Marion slowed down and impatiently ushered the runner ahead of her, all but pushing him toward home plate. Her team nearly always won.

Marion enjoyed playing baseball, which pleased her mother; she had been looking for an outlet for her spirited daughter. Then one day, as her mother tells it, she came to bat late in a game she had dominated.

"Hit her between the eyes!" a parent of a player on the opposing team called out.

"Bean her!" another adult called, and soon a number of the

spectators, grown men and women, were yelling at the pitcher to throw the ball at the girl standing at the plate with a bat in her hand.

"If this keeps up, somebody is going to prison here," Marion's stepfather, Ira Toler, told her mother. "We have to find something else for her to do."

Marion was enrolled in a gymnastics class the next week, and never played baseball in an organized league again.

On Saturday mornings, Marion's brother, Albert, would try to sneak out of the house early and alone, but he seldom made it. Marion, who was five years younger, was almost always waiting for him to go meet his friends.

Dolls? Marion never wanted one. Dresses? Girlfriends? Marion had little interest. It was Albert she cared about. Albert, his friends, and their games. All their games. Baseball, basketball, bike riding, hide-and-go-seek, every variation of tag—they were all part of the weekend routine, and Marion didn't want to miss any of it.

"I was really quite annoying," Marion said of those early-morning forays with Albert into their neighborhood in Palmdale, a high-desert community in the Antelope Valley north of Los Angeles. "He's trying to hang out with his friends and his little sister is with him. He'd say, 'Mom, does Marion have to come?' and she would say, 'Just let her tag along, she's not going to be in the way.' I was in the way, of course, but I think he got used to it after a while."

Albert got used to it when he and his friends discovered that even though Marion was playing with boys, some considerably bigger than she was, she could more than hold her own.

"Even when she was six years old," said Albert, a real estate appraiser in the Pacific Ocean community of Oxnard, "she could compete with my friends and me. She could dribble a basketball, run races with us, ride bikes with us. She could throw a baseball, and hit one. When it came to games, she didn't have any girl-like qualities. It was almost like having a brother."

As for any of Albert's friends who might grumble about playing with a girl, the point soon became moot. There was little any of them could say after Marion had won another game of 21, or another race around the block.

"Hey, my sister is beating all you guys," Albert would crow after Marion had won another game of pickle, a game in which a runner would try to avoid being tagged out by players throwing a baseball back and forth between two trees.

After a time, Marion's playtime presence among the neighborhood boys was no longer unusual. Soon, she was among the first chosen when they divided into teams, and, no matter what game was being played, Albert made sure he was a captain so he could choose his sister. "She was strong, almost as tall as most of my friends," he said, "and she never, ever quit."

Marion's greatest triumph in Palmdale came when Albert and his friends made a ballot box and conducted a neighborhood vote for their whiffle ball All-Star team. Marion, who was seven, was among those chosen.

"That was one of the most exciting moments of my short life," she said, grinning at the memory.

It was soon clear that Marion would not be able to enjoy sports, or to get better at them, unless she played against boys exclusively. She was the tallest girl in her kindergarten and first-grade classes and simply too fast and strong for the others.

"When they put her in a girls race at school, she smoked them," Albert said. "It was just no competition. When most girls are growing up, they play with other girls, and if they get into sports, that's who they compete against. With Marion, it was different. She competed against boys because she had to."

"Little girls were too soft for her," Marion's mother said. "She had to play with the boys."

But just playing with boys wasn't enough; very early, Marion discovered how much she liked beating them. She liked how it felt being on the winning team, crossing the finish line first, coming home from school or youth-group play days with medals. And if winning meant working even harder, fine. When Albert showed her how to shoot a jump shot, she stayed out on the court practicing until her mother insisted she come inside. In gymnastics class, when she saw older girls practicing back flips, cartwheels, or handstands, she asked an instructor to demonstrate and, within a month, she was doing them as well as the older girl next door, who had been practicing for years. Not long after that, she was doing them almost as well as the instructor.

Marion's capacity for learning a skill or technique, and then practicing until she had mastered it, was one she never lost, and one that never failed to impress her coaches in high school, college, and beyond.

Once, Marion asked Albert how he ran so fast, ignoring the fact that he was thirteen and she was eight. He had been copying what he saw on television, Albert told her, and soon they were both down on the ground practicing the sprinter's crouch and starting burst. Neither of them knew precisely what they were doing, of course, but they did know there was more to running than simply letting their legs fly. Marion ran from a crouch from then on.

Another quality Marion began to develop at a very young age is one she considers crucial to her athletic success. Sylvia Hatchell, her basketball coach at the University of North Carolina, calls it focus, the ability to concentrate exclusively on the job at hand, and says Marion possessed it to an extraordinary degree. Marion calls it living in the moment.

"I was never really interested in boys, but I didn't have girlfriends, either," she said. "I was always interested in whatever we were doing at the time. I remember certain moments of hide-and-go-seek. I remember certain moments of playing pickle. I remember falling when I was climbing down from the elementary school roof and scraping up my leg and lying to my mom, telling her I'd fallen off my bike. But I can't really remember one specific moment with a friend. I really can't. Not as a child."

There was something else Marion possessed at a young age, and the memory of it still amazes her mother and her brother. From the very beginning, she had an extraordinary sense of confidence.

Watching the wedding of Prince Charles and Diana Spencer on television in 1981, she was fascinated by the pomp and ceremony that attended the royal couple.

"Why do they roll out a red carpet for them?" she asked.

"They roll it out for very important people," her mother replied.

"Well, when I go places," Marion said, "why don't they roll it out for me?"

Amazing, Albert thought. She was only five years old, but already she was envisioning greatness for herself.

. . .

SOON MARION'S NEIGHBORHOOD games gave way to more organized activities—basketball, T-ball, volleyball, soccer, gymnastics, track, ballet, tap dancing, the Brownies. Her mother and stepfather saw her passion for play and made the most of it. By the time Marion was seven, she was a veteran competitor in the 100-yard dash and the 400 at organized track meets. To Marion, these meets were little different from running around the block with Albert and his friends. The feeling of winning a race was very much like the feeling of beating her brother to the base, or outrunning a throw.

Still, there were certain things even a seasoned, supremely confident seven-year-old had to get used to. At one meet, Marion won her heat in the 400 and waited to be crowned the winner. Then it was announced she had finished third. Marion ran crying to her mother and stepfather in the stands. She had won her race, she told them as the tears ran down her face. She had done what they told her to do. Her stepfather took her down to the track and asked one of the officials to explain that winning the heat didn't mean winning the race, which was based on best overall time.

"They explained it but it didn't make me feel any better," Marion said. "I didn't get the gold that day. I'll always remember that, and I'll always remember running in these big high-top shoes. They felt like they went up to my shins and I was just running and running.

"I was always on the move, always on the go. I had to be doing something. It was such a wonderful time of my life. There were no pressures and I had my family around me. That was the best part. I had such a loving family."

MARION JONES'S MOTHER, Marion Toler, was born in Belize, then known as British Honduras, and her first memories are of living in a place called Regalia on the banks of the Sittee River, which flowed through the jungle. Her father was a *chiclero,* who grew the plants from which chewing gum is made, and he hunted wild hogs, deer, and partridge, and grew vegetables on his land.

George Hulse built the family's thatched-roof home with his hands, and everything in it came from the forest. The kitchen floor was the mud of the riverbank and, because the Sittee was brackish, fresh water came from a spring to which his wife, son, and daughter paddled in a canoe. In the evenings the little girl would walk outside, gaze at the mountains in the distance, listen to the birds, and yell just to hear her echo.

The images of those early days in the jungle—of the jaguar sitting at her front door, of the golden sun setting in the evening—remain vivid to Marion's mother. Even now, thirty years after she left Belize, when it would be convenient to have a U.S. passport to travel to Australia to see her daughter run in the Olympics, she has never become an American citizen.

Hulse's family descended from Belize's original aristocrats, but had long since squandered its inheritance. Years later his daughter laughed when she saw the movie *Titanic* and its depiction of the girl and her mother who had lost their fortune and were living on their name. It is still that way with her father's family back in Belize, she thought. Rich or poor, if you're a Hulse, you're special.

Marion Hulse idolized her mother, Eva, though she was too young to understand her mother's sense of morbidity. "Behave yourself," she would tell Marion, "because when I die you're going to have a wicked stepmother who's going to be mean to you." She would die, Eva said, when she was forty years old.

Eva Hulse died when she was forty-three. Sure of her fate, she had long since made all the preparations for her funeral, even designating where to obtain the lumber for her coffin. Her daughter, who was eight years old, remembered all of this.

By this time, the family had left the banks of the Sittee, where there were no schools for Marion and her brother, Godwin, and moved to Eva's hometown of Maskall. Eva's death left George Hulse, no longer a young man, faced with a decision. He had promised Eva he would see the children through high school, but there was no free education in Belize, and no work for him away from the jungle.

He would move to Guatemala, he decided, try to earn a living there, and send money back for the children. They would stay with distant relatives and he would visit when he could. So in a short time, his young son and daughter were left to feel abandoned twice. "That was tough," Marion Toler recalled years later. "I really missed my dad a lot."

Eva's warning came true in other ways, too. Though the relative Marion was living with was not really her stepmother, Marion felt very much like Cinderella.

Marion was so stupid, her guardian told her again and again. Why did her father waste money on sending her to school? And she was ugly, too. No man would ever marry her. All she was good for was work, from morning till night, with time out for school only because the nuns would wonder where she was. "She made sure I had enough chores so I would be late for school," Marion said. "I was late every day for ten years. I hold the record."

There were beatings, too, with sticks and firewood, anything that came to hand. And within a year, Marion and Godwin, who had been raised in the Anglican church, had been baptized as Catholics. When she asked her father on one of his visits about this arrogant act, he turned the other cheek. "It's the same God for all Christians," he said. "And I knew the Catholics have money and you'd have a good education."

Marion did receive a good education and she made the most of it. She grew into a tall, graceful woman with a passion for conversation and an infectious laugh. She became a secretary, and then a legal secretary. Years later she would be able to get well-paying jobs that she enjoyed and that gave her family security.

The morning of her graduation—her guardian made sure she was late for that, too—one of the nuns told her father what a good student she was, how smart and hardworking.

"She isn't smart," her guardian insisted. "You ought to meet her brother. He's the smart one."

"I can only speak of Marion," the nun replied. "She's my best."

Later, when she came to America, she often thought how much she wished she could have learned to play the piano. When she had children, she promised herself, they would learn to play the piano. Or they could do other things, whatever they wanted. There would be no limits to what they could do.

IRA TOLER WAS a retired postal worker and World War II veteran who doted on his young stepdaughter. Marion Jones, for her part, clung to Ira fiercely and couldn't imagine life without him.

Ira was as much a mother to Marion as a father. While Big Marion—the nickname was given to Marion's mother by her daughter's friends and coaches—was off in Los Angeles or Beverly Hills working as a legal secretary, Ira took care of things at home.

He cooked, cleaned, shopped, took Marion to T-ball practice

and track meets, helped with her homework, and had dinner on the table when her mother returned from her long commute into the city. When Marion came home from school for lunch, Ira had her favorite macaroni and cheese ready, or sometimes he showed up unannounced at school with a McDonald's cheeseburger and fries while the other kids were eating cafeteria food.

"Whenever he went somewhere, whether it was to the store or to the lodge to hang out with his buddies, I'd be right there," Marion said. "It was almost like I was living in his back pocket."

Having come from a big family himself, Ira was much taken by Marion's excitement about everything she did. Albert often thought Marion reminded Ira of his own youth and made him feel young himself.

One day, Albert drove his sister to ballet practice on his bicycle and they took a tumble. Marion came home with her tights and tutu torn, her ballet slippers badly scuffed, and, worst of all, the bag she had begged her mother to buy for her tap shoes ripped apart.

"Little girl, you keep on scraping up your knees and your legs like that, they're not going to want you to be a model," Ira said, and he gave her a hug.

Then, when Marion was eleven years old, Ira died of a stroke. Brokenhearted, she could feel her life changing in ways she did not completely understand. She had yearned for a father figure and Ira had been that and so much more. He was the man who raised her, who took care of her, who loved her. But now she had to face the fact that despite her love for him, something had been missing.

"I loved Ira to death," she said, "but he was not my real dad."

• • •

MARION'S MOTHER MET George Jones in 1972 at one of the laundromats he owned in Los Angeles where she took her clothes. When, after a year of casual conversation, he began to court her, she was wary. She had already had one bad marriage, to Albert Kelly, her son's father, not long after she had emigrated from Belize to New York. She had always wondered if she had acted in haste because of the memory of the woman she had lived with telling her no one would marry her.

Kelly was twenty years older, and now here she was becoming interested in another man well into his forties. Her father had been quite a bit older than her mother and she wondered if she instinctively associated older men with kindness and maturity. But Jones was a nice-looking man, had his own business, and was a Louisiana Creole, which amused her because back home she had been known as a Belize Creole. "In my deficient state at the time, I was thinking, 'Creole man, Creole woman. It's a start,'" she said.

Jones wanted to get married right away and would not be put off when she said they should wait awhile. Once again, her guardian's voice haunted her. You're ugly, the voice said. Nobody will ever love you. And there was Albert, who needed a father.

Two weeks after Jones moved Marion and her son into a large house in Hollywood, he packed up and left without a word. Fortunately, she had her job, which forced her to at least *try* to stop crying for part of the day, but she had to move out of the fancy house and find an apartment.

"Don't take him back," Jones's sister told her. "Do you hear what I'm telling you? Don't take him back. Do you know what he did to his first wife? Lovely woman. He waited until she was gone and he broke up their entire house. He'll do the same thing to you."

She took him back and they moved into a house he bought on the border of Beverly Hills. In October 1975 her daughter, Marion Jones, was born.

George Jones disappeared and came back many times. Some days his wife would come into the house and find his closets empty. Later he would return without a word.

"Wrong? There ain't nothin' wrong," he would growl when she asked. "I just got a headache, that's all."

"I was the headache," she said.

She looked for a way out. She had been through ten years of hell as a child and she was not going to have her children living the same way. And besides, there were things she could do. She was a legal secretary. She worked for lawyers. She understood the system.

They separated and she forced Jones to pay the mortgage on the house and child support. Often, he would bring twenty-five dollars in pennies, nickels, and dimes from the laundromat, and she and the children would go to the bank to get wrappers to roll them in.

One night she came home and found the entire house torn apart. There were gaping holes in the windows and doors, and the furniture had been trashed. Jones had broken the toilet tank and garbage disposal with a crowbar and had even cut the plug off the refrigerator cord. Then, realizing how easily it could be fixed, he had stabbed the freezer with an ice pick.

She quickly got a divorce and forced him to sign over the house. There were advantages, it turned out, to working for good, no-nonsense Beverly Hills attorneys. It wasn't easy working and raising two young children, but she had a good job and was able to keep things together.

Then Ira Toler came along and she got her kids out of the city to the cleaner air and safer streets of Palmdale. She was lucky, she thought, and she was rid of George Jones.

LITTLE MARION COULDN'T understand it. If you had a daughter, if she visited you regularly during the years she was growing up, if she even lived with you several days a week for a short time when she was in junior high school, how could she be so unimportant to you? Why wouldn't you go to her high school graduation? Why wouldn't you go to her sports awards banquets when you had said you would? Why would you promise to go to New Orleans, your hometown, to share in her excitement at running in the U.S. Olympic trials when she was sixteen years old, and then not come? Why, when she was about to travel across the country to go to college, would you pretend not to be at your laundromat when she came to visit you?

"I'd see him in the back when I was pulling up," Marion said. "Then I'd go to his office and he wouldn't open the door. Or someone who worked for him would say, 'He was just here. I wonder where he went.' That happened three times."

Complicating matters was the fact that when Ira died, Albert was living in Belize with an uncle. This meant that Marion, who had once had three men in her life, now had none. If he had been around, Albert thought, the blow might have been cushioned somewhat. But in the end, he believed the circumstances might have served to make Marion stronger. "You can gain a lot of strength when you have to solve your own problems," he said.

Still, there were times when the cost seemed terribly high. Marion would become envious when she saw other little girls playing with their fathers. She knew her mother loved her, and

Marion loved her back, but there was something missing, Marion thought.

"I know that if I'd had my dad around, I would have been a daddy's girl."

IN MARCH OF 1995 the University of North Carolina's women's basketball team played in the Western Regionals of the NCAA tournament at UCLA. When the team returned to the floor from the locker room for the second half, Marion looked up into the stands and was startled to see her father. After the game she came back to the court to see if he had waited for her, but he was gone.

# 2

When Melissa Johnson enrolled at the University of North Carolina, she discovered an odd phenomenon.

"Every time somebody mentioned Marion's name," said Melissa, who had been a high school basketball star back home in Syracuse, New York, "they'd half whisper it. And there would be a three-second pause between the 'Marion' and the 'Jones.' All I could think was, This girl must be something else."

Marion and her family and friends were used to this by then. It had been going on almost from the moment she got to high school.

IN 1990, DURING HER freshman year at Rio Mesa High School in Oxnard, Marion rode with the track team to the Arcadia Invitational, a well-established meet that prided itself on bringing in many of the best high school athletes in California, and occasionally some top performers from around the country as well.

It was Marion's first meet against runners not just from nearby schools, and her first competition at night. After taking the long bus ride, walking into the floodlit football stadium, and seeing the packed stands, Marion could feel the excitement. So this is the big time, she thought.

The star of the evening was Inger Miller, a senior at Muir High in Pasadena, the daughter of former Olympic sprinter Lennox Miller and one of the top high school runners in the country. Inger beat Marion by a step in both the 100 meters and the 200 and was named Athlete of the Meet.

"It's a good thing you beat her now," said a meet official, stunned that a mere freshman had come so close, as he handed Inger the trophy, "because I don't think you will ever beat her again."

Later that spring, Marion won the first two of her nine California high school track championships in a state meet Inger Miller missed because of an injury. The following year, the Arcadia Invitational had another senior waiting for her: Zundra Feagin of Florida, the 1990 High School Athlete of the Year.

"I thought it was exciting because they were paying so much attention to women's events," Marion said, and the idea that an athlete would be brought in all the way from Florida made the meet feel like a national championship. Marion left Zundra well up the track, running the 200 in 22.87 seconds, the second fastest time in history by a high school girl. She beat her in the 100 as well.

"It was a stunning performance," said Doug Speck, the director of the meet. "I think it was her first big breakthrough on the track. To bring out this girl from Florida, who had run better times than she had, and to have Marion beat her twice was an amazing thing."

Not long afterward, Marion won her third and fourth state high school sprint titles and the first of an unprecedented three awards as National High School Athlete of the Year.

BEFORE THE START of Marion's freshman basketball season, Al Walker, the Rio Mesa coach, noticed her speed and the spring in her legs and asked if she could jump up and touch the bottom of the net. Marion did so easily, and Walker, who was talking to an assistant coach and not paying close attention, turned back to her and asked if she could touch the backboard as well.

Marion said she thought she could and as Walker resumed his conversation, she jumped up and slapped the backboard. Walker heard the sound and turned his full attention on Marion. Could she touch the rim? he asked

"Now bear in mind," Walker said, "this is a fourteen-year-old girl. When I was an eleventh- or twelfth-grader, my buddies and I would hang around after practice to see if any of us could jump up and touch the rim. We'd say, 'I touched it.' 'No, you didn't.' 'Well I touched the hook.' 'Yeah, you touched the hook. Big deal.' This is the hook the net hangs from. So that's what I was thinking when I asked her if she could touch the rim."

Marion walked to the top of the circle, ran around the three-point arc, turned toward the basket as she reached the baseline, came across the floor, and jumped.

"She didn't touch the rim," Walker said. "She *grabbed* it. She was above the basket. She was *well* above the basket. All I could do was turn to my assistant and say, 'Did you see that?'"

During Marion's freshman season, when she averaged 24.5 points and more than eleven rebounds per game, Walker would occasionally tease her by saying she might become the first high school girl ever to dunk the ball during a game. Marion would just laugh and say no, she didn't think so. But Walker would persist.

"If you do dunk the ball," he said, "you'd better make sure it's against a team we're going to beat because I'm going to get up off the bench, walk outside, pay admission, and watch the rest of the game from the stands." Marion never dunked the ball at Rio Mesa and Walker kept his seat on the bench.

IN THE SUMMER of 1991, after her sophomore year at Rio Mesa, Marion's mother managed to raise $2,500 to send her on a dream trip. Marion had been attending a weekend basketball camp run by Mel Sims, a respected coach in Pasadena who occasionally took all-star teams on goodwill visits to the Far East. This time, they would compete against high school teams in Hong Kong and then cross the border into China for a few days.

During a game in the Chinese city of Shenzhen, an errant pass sailed high over Marion's head, and she raced down the court and caught the ball just as she was flying out of bounds behind the basket. Without looking, she threw the ball back over her head to a teammate, landed beyond the baseline, reversed her momentum, turned around, came back onto the court, took the return pass, and scored.

"I've been coaching basketball for thirty years," Sims said, "and I've never seen that before. It was one of those three or four plays in your life that you'll always remember."

The Chinese crowd buzzed with amazement at Marion's feat and the public-address announcer's translator, who didn't know much English himself, turned to Sims and said, "Whoosh!"

"Yes," Sims said, raising a finger. "Number one high school girl."

"Number one?"

"Number one track girl. California state champion."

The translator huddled with the announcer, who relayed the news to the crowd, with a slight embellishment. Number one runner in America, he said.

"They had to stop the game for almost ten minutes," Sims said. "The people went crazy. I've never seen an ovation like that."

The team remained in Shenzhen for a few more days and wherever it went it was accompanied by dozens, hundreds, and—on one occasion outside a factory it was visiting—thousands of people. Those who had heard about the game simply tagged along behind Marion and the others, following her wherever they went. To Sims, it seemed as if they just wanted to touch her, shake her hand, get her autograph. Equally amazing, the coach thought, was how Marion never seemed to tire of the attention.

"We'd be walking through the streets," Marion said, "and little kids would be coming up to us, never having seen black people in their lives, and rubbing our skin to see if the color would come off. We all had a ball."

AL WALKER WAS AMONG the first coaches to see Marion's intensity before a game. As the tip-off drew near, she would become very quiet and stare straight ahead, gathering her thoughts. Her teammates would notice and follow suit. Walker believed they were bothered more by the thought of letting her down than of losing the game. After a time, Walker came up with a name for Marion's stare, which others would notice over the years whenever she was preparing to compete. He called it the look of an assassin.

A couple of years later, after transferring to another school, her team lost the California Interscholastic Federation Southern Sectional championship game by one point when, following a hotly disputed foul, the other team made two foul shots after the buzzer.

Her coach tried to console the players by telling them they'd had a fine season and had nothing to be ashamed about. As he was leaving the locker room, he heard a loud *THWACK* against the door he had just closed.

"Marion took the case that held the runner-up medal and smashed it against the door," said Melissa Wood, one of her teammates. "Nobody wanted to pick it up, either. When we left, it was still on the floor."

MARION SOON CAME to expect big things of herself, and she had little patience for anything else. In 1991, when she was fifteen years old and a sophomore at Rio Mesa, her times in the sprints were fast enough for her to qualify for the U.S National Track and Field Championships, at Randalls Island, New York, against some of the best runners in the world. But rather than feeling awed at the company she was keeping, or even nervous, Marion surprised herself by how calmly she reacted. Perhaps she was too young to realize the huge competitive step up she was taking, but to her it felt like just another race.

"I remember lining up in the blocks and looking to my right and seeing Evelyn Ashford," Marion said, "then looking to my left and seeing Gwen Torrence. I had some butterflies, but when I got into the blocks I felt very focused and calm. I thought, 'All right, Evelyn, all right, Gwen, watch out now.'"

Marion finished sixth in the 100 and fourth in the 200, barely missing a place on the U.S. team that went to the World Championships in Tokyo that year. "I saw how fast I had run and how fast they had run," she said, "and I knew I could be right with them. I knew it wouldn't be long."

CHARLES BROWN, THE COACH of the Thousand Oaks High School basketball team, was recovering from quadruple-bypass heart surgery when the mother of one of his players, Melissa Wood, called with exciting news. She and Melissa had run into Marion and her mother at the school and they had asked to see him. She might be thinking of transferring from Rio Mesa.

Surely not, Brown thought. But then again why would Marion and her mother have come to school on a Sunday when their presence wouldn't be widely noticed? They must have something in mind. Brown went to his office the next day and found that Marion and her mother had been back asking for an enrollment form.

"I started to get well in a hurry," he said. "That was some of the best medicine I could have had."

Marion had been happy at Rio Mesa High, an ethnically mixed school where her friends provided a welcome relief from the pressures she was feeling at being one of California's best and most publicized high school athletes. Walker, the Rio Mesa basketball coach, had noticed that Marion's dedication to sports sometimes denied her the opportunity to be what he called a "full-on kid." Several times in the years ahead, Marion and her mother would tell him she had been happier at Rio Mesa than at upper-crust, and almost totally white Thousand Oaks.

"I'd gotten used to my friends at Rio Mesa and the transition didn't go very well," Marion said. "Besides my teammates, I didn't feel really comfortable with many of the students at Thousand Oaks. It was never a racial thing. It was more economic, I guess."

Her mother thought Rio Mesa, with its mixture of black, white, and Latino students, was perfect for her. But there was never any question about Marion transferring. The reason was simple: There were greater athletic opportunities at Thousand Oaks.

"Sports outweighed everything else," Marion said. "Many times, students transfer because of an academic problem. My problem was with sports. My mom saw my eyes light up when I was going to a track meet or to a basketball game. I was a different person when it came time for sports."

The seeds of the transfer were sown when Marion began working out with Elliott Mason, a psychologist and counselor at Los Angeles Harbor College who had been Olympic sprint champion Evelyn Ashford's running partner. Marion's mother was impressed when Mason's first concern was for her health. He sent Marion to an orthopedist who took X rays and measured her joints to see if she had stopped growing. Mason seemed interested in Marion as a person, not simply as an athlete, her mother thought. She liked that.

Mason often drove long distances to supervise Marion's workouts. Since Rio Mesa track coach Brian FitzGerald was only allowed to work with Marion during the track season, and since the 1992 Olympic trials were coming up, she and her mother felt she needed more coaching.

Marion and her mother asked FitzGerald to allow Mason to attend track practice at Rio Mesa. She would continue to run on the school team, but Mason would observe, make suggestions, and occasionally put her through some private drills. FitzGerald refused. "He told me that he absolutely would not work with any-body else," Marion's mother said. "He said she would not run on his track. *His* track? It was a public school."

FitzGerald admitted he was insulted by the idea that he work with another coach. Hadn't Marion won four state sprint championships under his coaching? Hadn't she run some of the fastest times in history for a girl her age? Why did she need another coach?

Art Green, the track coach at Thousand Oaks, had no such concern. His father, Donald Green, had coached Olympic pole vault champion Bob Seagren in high school and had been humbled by the experience. You don't use your association with great athletes to further yourself, his father had told him. Green had sometimes heard people talk about Seagren while his father remained silent about the part he had played in helping a scrawny high school boy get his start in track.

Besides, working with Mason proved not to be a problem. Rather than separate Marion from the team, Green simply added Mason to his coaching staff. The two men worked well together, Marion's performances improved, and Thousand Oaks suddenly had one of the best track teams in the state.

"There was never any conflict," Marion said. "Looking back, the fact that Coach Green didn't have a problem with Elliott actually surprises me a little bit. But there are people out there who are totally for the good of the kid."

Marion also flourished as a basketball player at Thousand Oaks. Rio Mesa's team had improved in her two years, but Al Walker knew it would not contend for the league championship for at least one more year. At Thousand Oaks, by contrast, Marion joined one of the best teams in the state. She also played for a coach who wasn't in awe of her.

Born in Kentucky and well traveled, Charles Brown had coached at Missouri Baptist College in St. Louis before moving to California, hiring on at Thousand Oaks as a science teacher, and later becoming coach of the girls' basketball team. Brown has the spare leathery look of a coaching lifer; when a film crew came to the school to shoot a commercial for Energizer batteries featuring the boys' basketball team, Brown was hired to play the coach. It was because he didn't look like an actor, Brown was told, and soon he was getting calls from former players asking, "Was that you in that commercial? Cool."

Brown was fifty-seven when Marion arrived at Thousand Oaks, a fact that may have played a part in her instant trust in him. That and his no-nonsense approach.

"I've never been really good dealing with men who want to be a father figure to me," Marion said. Coach Brown was hardnosed. It didn't matter that she was the highest-scoring player on the team, if she didn't do something right in practice or in school, he would make her run laps like all the others, no questions. That's what she liked about him.

What Brown liked about Marion was the way she fit into an already excellent team without trying to take over. Michelle Palmisano, who went on to play at UCLA and Vanderbilt, was the star, and Brown was alert to the possibility of conflict, but he never found any. Michelle continued her role as point guard while Marion, at five ten the tallest girl on the team, worked under the basket or out on the wing, and delighted Brown with her urge to lead.

"She would yell, 'Come on, now, pick up your girl over there,' or point where the play should go," he said. "A lot of times a player can get more out of a team than a coach can because she's on their level. And when they see a great athlete putting out that kind of effort, they think, 'Well, hey, we've got to do it, too.'"

THE MORE MARION COMPETED in both sports during high school, the more the word got around about her talent. Art Green, the Thousand Oaks track coach, remembered a meet at Cal Poly Pomona her senior year when the runners lined up for the 100 meters and it seemed as if everyone in the stands moved forward to the rails. Then, after Marion had won, they all went back to their seats. "I'd never seen that before," Green said. "They just wanted to watch her. It was a phenomenon."

Charles Brown recalled the night the parent of a girl on another team showed up at one of Thousand Oaks' games—even though they weren't playing his daughter's team—just to see Marion play. Another time, a rival coach approached Brown and frankly admitted his game plan: stop Marion. A few hours later, after Marion had scored thirty-eight points with thirteen rebounds and eight blocked shots, the opposing coach shook his head. "We couldn't stop her," he told Brown.

Then there was the game at Rancho Bernardo, which Thousand Oaks was trailing, until, near the end, Marion drove from the right corner, dribbled under the basket, and made a reverse layup while her momentum carried her away from the hoop. Even Rancho Bernardo's fans went wild, Brown recalled. "You just don't see that very often," Brown said. It was something he would not forget.

But sometimes Marion's success bore unintended consequences for other young athletes, particularly opponents. Parents would occasionally approach Doug Speck after a race, worried that their daughters had no talent for track. "I'd say, 'No, no, when you're ten meters behind Marion Jones, you're still pretty good.'"

A PICTURE TAKEN by a newspaper photographer when Marion was in high school shows her racing against boys. Marion is in the lead.

"Coach Green made her do it," said Heather Hanger, a hurdler at Thousand Oaks who ran relays with Marion. "She ran with us some of the time, but for the harder workouts she had to run with the guys. We couldn't compete with her. We couldn't even help her."

If you wanted to see runners giving their best effort, Heather said, you should have seen boys running against Marion. "They didn't want a girl to beat them, so it was pretty funny," she said. "We knew she was going to kick our butts anyway, so we were happy she was running with them."

One day Thousand Oaks traveled to a meet at Moorpark High, where Marion and several of her teammates sat out because of a rule limiting the amount of competition an athlete is allowed during the season. One of the girls brought a video camera and they were clowning around and singing songs when some boys on the home team approached.

"Come on, Marion, let's race," they said. "Let's see how fast you are."

"No, no," Marion said, smiling and joking back.

"You can't beat me," one of the boys said, flirting now, and egging her on.

"You're probably right," Marion said, acting humble and conciliatory as her teammates laughed and tried to determine how many of the teasing boys Marion could have embarrassed in front of their friends.

MARION'S HIGH SCHOOL COACHES all speak of her capacity for leadership and of the instinctive way her teammates would turn to her for guidance. But there were times when this quality went beyond the usual pep talks.

The Thousand Oaks track team had just completed a long day of qualifying for the league championships at Camarillo High School and had trudged half a mile to the bus that would take them home when suddenly there was a problem. A Thousand Oaks runner, Kim Robinson, had tied a girl from a rival school for ninth place in the 200-meter dash, and, since there were only nine lanes on the Camarillo track, one of them had to be eliminated from the next day's final. The only fair way to do it, meet officials decided, was to have a runoff.

The team had been at the meet for five or six hours. The runners were tired and ready to go home, but now they were told they had to wait while Kim got off the bus and returned to the track to break a tie for ninth place.

"Marion, who had easily qualified for everything she was competing in, got every athlete off that bus, the boys and the girls, marched them the half mile back to the track, and lined them up from the beginning of the 200 to the finish so they could cheer Kim on," remembered Jerry Sawitz, an assistant track coach at Thousand Oaks. "Kim won the race, of course. With everybody cheering for her like that, how could she not?"

Nor was Marion afraid to challenge things that seemed wrong to her, or dumb. Heather Hanger, who is now an assistant track coach at the school, remembered that in competitions before Marion arrived on the team, the girls always wore "dolphins," or extremely short jogging shorts.

"It was something that had gone on for years, I guess, and most of the girls were pretty uncomfortable in them," Heather said.

"We were just teenagers, you know, and they *were* short. And if you were five or ten pounds overweight, you were really uncomfortable.

"The first day Marion came to practice, she wore Spandex bicycle shorts underneath the dolphins. She didn't ask anybody, she just did it. It was all we could talk about. Everyone was whispering, 'Omigosh, she's going to get cut from the team.' And then we said, 'What are we *talking* about? They're going to cut *Marion* from the team? Come on.'

"So we all started wearing Spandex. First, it was just those of us on the relay team because our outfits had to match, but pretty soon everybody was wearing Spandex. And you know what happened? Nothing. Nobody said a word. The girls have worn Spandex ever since."

Now Heather is impressed that Marion won't wear "buns," the even shorter bikini bottoms that most top women track athletes wear, apparently on the theory that shorter is faster. Marion has never worn them, and she continues to wear the same long bicycle shorts that make her stick out on every starting line.

"If buns are so great," Marion said, "why aren't the men wearing them?"

WHEN MARION'S ACCOMPLISHMENTS on the track began to go national, so did the debate over her participation in two sports.

What was such a prodigiously talented young track star doing playing basketball, a sport that cut into her practice time and in which she could get hurt? track officials asked. If she wanted to realize her potential, if she wanted to go to the Olympics, she should be dedicating herself to track.

What was such a brilliant basketball player doing hiding her light under a low-profile bushel like track? came the counter-argument. Women's basketball was booming. That was the sport she should be concentrating on.

But Marion's high school coaches refused to take sides. "I've never told any kid to give up another sport for my sport," said Art Green, whose track team Marion reported to only after the basketball season had ended. "I don't think anybody has the right to do that. Besides, I loved watching her play basketball."

And in fact, state policy encouraged high school athletes to diversify. They are not allowed to train with their coaches out of season, explained Dean Crowley, the former commissioner of the California Interscholastic Federation (CIF), which meant she couldn't work with her track coach during basketball season anyway.

"Now she was going to participate in some activity after school, wasn't she?" Crowley asked. "So why not something she liked and did well? She was still just a girl."

"Look at what kids do evenings and weekends, skateboarding and all the rest of it," said Bob McGuire, a longtime coach and state track official. "They look at things differently. They just want to have fun."

Hal Harkness, the director of the state track meet in which Marion won nine titles over a four-year span, understood the argument. But as a track fan who was afraid the sport might never come to know what Marion could accomplish, he felt differently.

"To hell with basketball," Harkness said with a laugh. "We wanted to see her do track, track, track."

As they sat in the CIF offices in Orange County next to a large photo of Marion long jumping in her Thousand Oaks track uniform, Crowley, McGuire, and Harkness considered the many precocious high school athletes they had seen who had disappeared without a trace.

Burnout is a common phenomenon, they agreed, particularly among athletes who are pushed to high levels when they are young; competing just isn't fun anymore. For girls, it can be even more complicated: Their bodies change, they become interested in boys, they hear old wives' tales about how sports can affect childbearing. And even in this era of Title IX, the federal statute that mandates equal athletic opportunity, there is not always as much support for gifted young female athletes as there is for male athletes. By moving back and forth between sports, they agreed, Marion kept her feelings fresh for both of them.

"As convoluted as the path was," Harkness said, "in retrospect, it was the right path. You just wouldn't design it that way."

And in fact, Marion hadn't designed it. She had simply done what she wanted to do, what seemed right at the time. It was a quality that would assert itself often over the ensuing years. Instinctively, it seemed, the one person who knew what was right for Marion was Marion.

"'Why don't you decide? Why don't you decide?'" Marion recalled people asking her. "I thought, 'Why do I have to make that decision now?' I knew I wouldn't be able to continue doing them both at the same time, but when I'm fifty or sixty years old I want to be able to say I did what I wanted to do. I want to be able to say I was happy."

MIDWAY THROUGH HER junior season, in a basketball game at Simi Valley, Marion broke her wrist and dislocated her jaw. Though she had been diagnosed with a stress fracture in her left foot after her freshman year, it had quickly healed, so this was her first serious injury and the first indication of trouble ahead on several fronts.

The videotape of the play is horrifying to watch. Down near her own basket, Marion tips away an opponent's pass, grabs the ball, and sets off for the opposite end of the court. By the time she nears the basket, she is flying, and a defender has moved in to block her path. But rather than attempt to block the shot, or to guard Marion in any way, the defender does the one thing no competent basketball player would ever do.

She ducks.

Covering her head and crouching down as if she has heard a gunshot, she presents her back to Marion, who digs a knee into it and goes into an almost perfect somersault. Marion lands on her wrist and goes sprawling off the court.

"My face was going to hit the ground and to stop my fall I put my hand down, and it broke," Marion said. "Then I came down and hit my chin anyway and dislocated my jaw. I knew my hand was broken because it was really swollen. I could hardly see my fingers. But then I realized I couldn't talk. I couldn't move my mouth. That's what scared me because I didn't know what had happened to my jaw."

Marion had broken two bones in her wrist, the radius and the ulna, and later at the hospital it took half a dozen tries to set them.

"I was just screaming, screaming, screaming," she said. "I said, 'At least tell me what you're doing so I can prepare myself.' Then, when they finally got them in place and took me to the X-ray room, this lady was moving me around like nothing was wrong. I said, 'I have a broken wrist here. Can you please take it a little easy?'"

Visiting Marion in the hospital before she went home that night, Melissa Wood was appalled at how groggy the painkillers had made her. Later Melissa told her how she had gone in to shoot the free throws Marion had been in no condition to take. "I dribbled the ball four times because she was number forty-four," Melissa said. "It was a real sentimental thing for me, so I did it forever after that. I made the shots, too."

Some of the fallout from Marion's injury was not pleasant. See what she gets for playing basketball? some track and field officials said. And only six months before the Olympic trials, too.

"I heard one comment that really angered me," Charles Brown said. "Supposedly, a basketball official from the area said, 'Thousand Oaks got what they deserved, because they bought her.' I confronted him and he claims he didn't say that. A couple of other people said he did."

But the most hurtful moments were private ones between Marion and her mother. They began the night she came home from the hospital and went to bed on the second floor of their town house. If she needed anything, her mother told her—a drink of water, anything—just call her and she'd bring it. But when Marion, independent as ever, woke up, she decided to go downstairs to get a drink for herself. She almost made it, before slipping in the dark and banging her newly broken arm against the wall.

"I told you! I told you!" her mother said as she came rushing downstairs to comfort Marion, who sat on the bottom step, screaming in pain.

The tension persisted for weeks as Marion became sullen and uncommunicative, which left her mother distraught.

"I kept it bottled in," Marion said. "She never really knew how

I was feeling because I wouldn't tell her. Here I was going through puberty, still bitter about the whole dad situation, and taking it out on my mom, simply because she was my mom. I was miserable to deal with."

"She *was* miserable," her mother said. "I couldn't do anything for her. I stopped working. I stayed at home to nurse her, cook her favorite food, help her down the stairs. But she didn't want me to."

The crux of the problem was obvious. For the first time in her life, Marion was unable to compete in sports, and she had nothing to replace them with. Going to practice just to watch was too frustrating to bear. So was using the time to study or hang out with friends. When people asked if there was *anything* other than sports she enjoyed doing, she didn't think the question was worth considering. Later, though, she had to admit that they had a point. That was not a good time for her, she thought. If it ever happened again, she would need something else in her life to fill the void.

Four years later, when she suffered two serious foot injuries in college, Marion remembered those thoughts and could only laugh. She was, she realized, just as depressed and miserable as she had been in high school.

"When I was in high school, the stakes were high to me," Marion said. "And in college, I had a team that relied on me. I wasn't making money, but it was my life."

Even today, she does not respond well to enforced inactivity. When her back was sore early in the 1999 season and she had to take a couple of days off from practice, she was antsy. "I was touchy, I was striking back," she said. "It's probably always going to be that way with me, even though I know it shouldn't. It's different now, but I think it will always hurt about the same."

After six weeks of inactivity, Marion asked the doctor to remove the cast. Reluctantly, he agreed and wrapped her injured wrist in a brace. Take it easy, he warned her. Marion immediately returned to the basketball team. Every time she touched the ball, she could feel shivers through her entire body, but she wouldn't say anything for fear her mother or the coach would insist she stop playing. And besides, the injury was hardly affecting her performance. In a tournament game, Marion scored thirty points and had nineteen rebounds and nine blocked shots. Because she had missed almost all of Thousand Oaks' conference games, she wasn't named to the all-league team, so she had to settle for all-county and all-state honors instead.

In 1996, when Marion broke her foot while working out on a trampoline at the University of North Carolina, Charles Brown sent her a puckish note reminding her of that first serious injury. "To me," he wrote, "it's the sign of a person who just doesn't have much coordination."

ONE OF THE THINGS that amazed Marion's high school coaches was her poise in public. Art Green's phone rang constantly with calls from reporters asking for interviews, and when, as a junior, Marion tried out for the U.S. Olympic team, the press attention became even more intense. But after monitoring her first few interviews, Green lost all concern about whether she might need protection or guidance.

"She handled the press better than anybody I've ever seen," he said. "From the first time I saw her, she had it down. She was a natural. I would just send her over to whoever wanted to talk to her and she would have them wrapped around her little finger. They loved her to death."

Marion's brother, Albert, thinks Marion's natural way with the press comes from their mother, who often admonished them about talking without having much to say. "She would tell us, 'Don't just jump into what you're going to say, put some thought behind it,'" he said. Albert said Marion would pay keen attention to people who had that quality, whether it was a teacher defusing a tense situation, or people on the news who carried themselves well. She wanted to remember exactly what they were saying and how they were behaving.

Marion thinks her aplomb is natural. "Maybe it's because I've watched so many athletes come off as jerks, or be bland or stale," Marion said. "And I've never felt intimidated. In fact, the more people watching, and the more people asking questions, the more excited I get. This is my career and it's part of the job."

At Rio Mesa, where Al Walker was frank about using Marion to get publicity for a basketball team whose record would not otherwise warrant it, Marion's high visibility once caused a problem. Walker convinced a student reporter to do a story on the other players on the team, but when it was printed he realized he had overreached because Marion was portrayed as so superior to everyone else.

"We work our butts off and then we pick up the paper and it's all about Marion," one of her teammates said. "It's kind of hard to take."

Marion was the villain on campus for a few days and Walker was embarrassed at having created the problem. But he was impressed to see that Marion bore no animosity toward the reporter and that she seemed to have developed the maturity to know that the moment would pass. "I think a lot of that has to do with the exposure she got at a very early age," he said.

And besides, many of Marion's teammates enjoyed basking in the edges of the spotlight. "Every meet we went to, there were reporters and cameras," said Heather Hanger. "I think it was a little embarrassing to her because we all knew they weren't taking pictures of us. And she was very good about it, never snotty or standoffish."

Once, at the Mount San Antonio College Relays, which brings high school athletes onto the same track as some of the top performers in the world, the Thousand Oaks athletes were sitting together when they looked up and there was Carl Lewis.

"Hey, Marion," the Olympic sprint and long jump champion said.

"Oh, hi, Carl, what's up?" Marion said.

"Our jaws dropped," Heather said. "Nobody said anything for a while. We were all in shock."

But perhaps Marion's comfort level in public situations was at its highest when she was around children. Often, she spoke to youth track groups about hard work and staying in school. "It was amazing how she would have them in her grip," Art Green said, "how they would listen to her. These were kids from five to twelve years old and all the time I would be thinking she was only sixteen." Mel Sims invited her to come speak to his Pasadena basketball camp while she was still in college. Marion spoke off-the-cuff for thirty minutes about success and being motivated. Besides the way his campers looked at her with awe, Sims said he remembered one thing: "One of the kids came up to me afterwards and said, 'She is so nice.'"

This was a quality Marion had learned at home, and it expressed itself, Green said, in private moments as well as public ones.

In 1995 Green took his mother, who had always loved watching Marion compete, to see North Carolina play Stanford in the NCAA regional tournament at UCLA. Marion and her mother inquired after Green's father and were told he had died a few days earlier. The next day, a purple and white orchid arrived at Green's house.

"It was the nicest, most appropriate gift," he said. "It's in the backyard, in the original basket. It still blooms twice a year."

WHEN MARION WAS a junior, she won her fifth and sixth sprint titles at the California state high school track and field championships. Perhaps, she thought, as she entered her senior year, she should add another event. At dual meets during the season, she ran the 400 and the relays, and occasionally Art Green would see her practicing other events, as if she were trying them on for size.

She put the shot about thirty-nine feet the first time she tried the event, good enough, Green noted, to place in the CIF meet. The same was true of the high jump, in which she cleared the bar at well over five feet. One day, when Green wasn't watching, he heard a loud *CRACK*. Marion had been trying the hurdles and hit one with her knee.

"I turned to look and she was scampering off," Green said. "I knew that was probably her last time running the hurdles."

"I'm not much of one for pain," Marion said with a laugh. "It's hard enough running in a straight line."

Marion had become a huge fan of Carl Lewis and Jackie Joyner-Kersee, who were champion long jumpers as well as runners. Why not try that? she thought. From a practical point of view, Green thought it was a good idea because if she got off a good jump on her first try at the big state and sectional meets, she could pass on her remaining attempts—a common practice when jumpers think the other competitors won't catch them—and return to the sprints.

Despite knowing almost nothing about the mechanics of the event, Marion was soon jumping nineteen feet in practice, which put her among the top high school girls in the country. In her first competition, leaping into a pit that had been borrowed from a sand trap used for golf classes outside the stadium at Cal Poly Pomona, she jumped 19-10, the best in the nation by a high school girl to that point in the season. Green told her he thought she'd found her event.

"I didn't know what the heck I was doing," Marion said. "The pit was quite short and I nearly jumped on the grass. At that point, I really wasn't thinking about technique, just about winning and how far I could jump. It didn't matter how I looked."

Marion didn't practice the long jump much—her natural talent was enough for her to win—or compete at every meet. Still, Green thought it might eventually become her best event. She would need to learn to harness her speed as it continued to grow, and to master proper technique, but one day she might very well set a world record.

Green's one concern was the toll the long jump might take on Marion's other events. Jumping seemed to affect her sprinting, he thought, because it was hard on her legs. And since the long jump always preceded the sprints on meet schedules, he could see that she didn't have the same finishing kick afterward. Then, too, there was always the possibility of injury.

At the state meet her senior year, Marion's times in the sprints were, for the first time, slower than they had been the previous year. But she still won both races easily, and posted a mark of 22-0½ in the long jump, just short of a national high school record that had stood for thirteen years.

"She could have jumped twenty-three feet that day," said Green. "I blame it on the wind."

IN 1992 MARION's high school times were good enough to qualify for the U.S. Olympic trials. Though she was only sixteen, she was a veteran of the previous year's U.S. Nationals and had recovered nicely from her wrist injury. Her hopes were high as she went to the trials in New Orleans, and the possibility of going to the Games was exciting.

Marion was eight years old when she first became aware of the Olympics. The Games were in Los Angeles in 1984 and her family drove in from Palmdale to see the torch relay as it passed by. That evening Marion went to her room and wrote on her blackboard, "I want to be an Olympic champion."

Albert said that she went through the neighborhood for days telling people that one day she would be an Olympic champion and that they did not dismiss the idea as the unlikely dreams of a child. "They said, 'We believe you,'" he remembered.

As she saw the Games on television, Marion became even more enthralled. "I loved watching the athletes compete," she said. "I loved how overjoyed they got when they crossed the finish line first. I loved watching tears roll down their faces when they listened to their national anthems. The whole Olympic spirit was just so exciting to me."

This was Marion's first understanding that sports were not simply games for children, but could be an occupation, a lifetime pursuit. Competing in the Olympics became her goal. "I didn't know what sport it would be," Marion said. "I only knew I wanted to be great at it. No, not just great. The best."

Though Marion became infatuated with the beauty, grace, and versatility of Carl Lewis, she was also struck by something else. Everywhere she looked in the 1984 Games, she saw Evelyn Ashford and Jackie Joyner and Joan Benoit and Mary Lou Retton. Everywhere she looked, there were women.

"I was still a tomboy and I was still hanging out with my brother and his friends, but I was watching these women run fast and jump far and do all these wonderful things," she said. "They were so competitive and looked so strong and yet so beautiful, too. And they were so excited about what they were doing. That's what I wanted to be: confident, strong, graceful, intelligent. I wanted to be like them."

In 1988 the Olympics were in Seoul and Marion was back in front of her television set where she found herself fascinated by Florence Griffith Joyner. Everything about Florence—her strikingly colorful tracksuits, her long painted fingernails, her nonchalant poise, her lovely smile—made her the most charismatic track star in the world.

Earlier that summer, at the U.S. Olympic trials in Indianapolis, Florence had obliterated the world record in the 100-meter dash with a mark of 10.49, a record that has never been broken. At the Games in Seoul, she set a world record in the 200, 21.34, which also still stands.

"At that point, I didn't really grasp how fast she had run," Marion said. "I just knew that she looked like she was flying, like her feet never really hit the ground. I told my mom, 'This lady flies like the wind.'"

Marion ran well in New Orleans. Despite a heat so intense that some athletes passed out, she set a national high school record in the 200 that has yet to be equaled, and finished fourth, missing a spot on the team by seven one-hundredths of a second. She also finished sixth in the 100, which earned her a spot as an alternate on the 4×100-meter relay team in Barcelona. But after much agonizing, she and her mother agreed she should turn it down. Her mother was worried that things were happening too quickly, that she was simply too young. Marion had a different concern, that she wouldn't be allowed to run.

Alternates are often used in the early heats of relay competition—it takes an injury to get them into the finals—but Marion suspected that no coach would put her on the track with a gold medal on the line. She wasn't sure she would do it herself. "That's a lot for a sixteen-year-old," she said. "When you're talking about a gold medal in the Olympics, I don't know if I would have wanted that type of pressure. Obviously, my body wasn't mature and neither was my head."

But suppose she was entered in one of the early heats. The United States was almost certain to win the relay, and every member of the team, including those who ran only in the preliminaries, would receive gold medals. That clinched it as far as Marion was concerned. She wasn't going.

"Ever since I could remember, I wanted my first gold medal to be something that I sweated for," she said. "I didn't want anybody giving me one. People said, 'Are you guys crazy? You're going to pass up going to the Olympics for some silly nonsense like you might not run?'"

But for Marion, it was once again a case of living in the moment, and 1992 was somebody else's moment, not hers.

"I want to be an Olympic champion," she said. "I want gold

medals. But when I'm eighty years old and I'm sitting in my rocking chair on the veranda drinking lemonade with my husband, and my grandkids run up to me, I want to be able to show them my gold medals and say, 'See this, honey? This is something that I ran for, that I sweated for, that I earned. Nobody handed me this.'"

So Marion stayed home and watched the Olympics on television.

"I'm not going to lie," she said. "Watching the women compete, it hurt. It hurt knowing that I could have been there, knowing that I could have been involved in the Olympic spirit. But I got over it quick. I knew my time was going to come."

IN 1993, WHEN MARION was a senior in high school, she was suspended from national and international competition for missing a drug test. It was the beginning of a nightmare that threatened to destroy her track career just as it was getting started, and it gave Marion and her mother their first real understanding of what the politics of track and field could be like.

Once she began competing on a national level, Marion became subject to out-of-competition random drug testing. The procedure was for the Athletics Congress (TAC)—the sport's U.S. governing body, which later changed its name to USA Track & Field —to send an express letter directing an athlete to report to a testing site forty-eight hours later. In Marion's case, this meant leaving school and her mother taking time off from work to drive into Los Angeles.

Marion was training with Elliott Mason by then and her mother decided that rather than have an important-looking envelope lying outside their door all day while she was at work, all Marion's mail from TAC should be directed to Mason's office at

Harbor College. A letter delivered in September announcing Marion's next random drug test was tossed aside in the mail room, and by the time Mason received it, TAC had another message for Marion. She was suspended for four years.

"The minute Elliott got the letter he jumped on the phone," Marion's mother said, "but they didn't want to hear it. Not coming in for a drug test is like being guilty. She had committed a crime and they were going to punish her, make an example out of her. They came at us with both barrels."

The first time Marion knew the matter had gone public was when a classmate told her he had seen it in the newspaper. So much for trying to resolve privately what was clearly a misunderstanding. There was never any question that she had actually *failed* a drug test, after all. When the one she had missed was rescheduled, she passed, although the results were not officially announced.

"I didn't know what to do," Marion said. "I'm in high school, I'm beating everybody, I'm on cloud nine and all of a sudden it comes out in the papers that I'm suspended for four years. When people read things like that they don't see what it really says. All they see is drugs . . . suspended . . . four years."

The suspension did not keep Marion out of high school meets, but it did make her ineligible for important open competition at the Sunkist Invitational, an indoor meet in Los Angeles in January, and the Mount San Antonio College Relays in April. She ran in the high school portion of those meets instead, and even then there were frantic faxes and phone calls back and forth to make sure she was not breaking any rules. "They were upset about it," Art Green said of the meet promoters. "She had always done real well at Mount Sac."

For months Marion and her mother were left to their own devices to fight a powerful organization that seemed more interested in punishing a simple mistake than in dispensing justice.

"They had four powerhouse attorneys," said Marion's mother, who was referred to a lawyer of her own, who accomplished little other than submitting a bill for nearly ten thousand dollars. Things were getting out of control, she realized, and there was nothing she could do to stop them.

Then Johnnie Cochran entered the picture. Why would they want to harass a girl who so obviously didn't deserve it? the famous attorney, whose wife is Elliott Mason's cousin, asked when Marion and her mother went to his office. Look at all the stories about kids in trouble, kids in gangs, kids using drugs. Why destroy the future of an exemplary young woman?

"What they were doing was outrageous," Cochran said. "It was a violation of everything I would hold sacred. She didn't even have a hearing. She was just suspended and knocked out of all these meets at a critical time in her life."

Don Wilson, a lawyer in Cochran's office, began researching the case and was appalled at what he found. Not only did nobody ever win an appeal, but the mere *fact* of an appeal was held against you. Accepting the suspension meant it might be shortened after a year or so, but if an athlete lost there was no chance of an early reversal.

"I had to tell Marion that statistically and historically everything was against us, and with so much of her career ahead of her, it might be better to accept the suspension," Wilson said.

But Marion was determined to appeal. She was just a teenager. She had done nothing wrong. The TAC officials had to see that. "It was very brave of her," Wilson said. "It really could have harmed her career."

On a conference call with three TAC hearing officers, Wilson mounted two arguments. The first was that the letter to report for the drug test had not contained Elliott Mason's room number at Harbor College, although Marion had included it on a card she had filled out for TAC. The second was the arbitrary nature of the suspension process.

Wilson read one case that almost made him cry. Officials sent a testing notice to an athlete at his home while he was away competing for a U.S. team in Europe. He thought surely they would waive the notification rule since they knew where he was, he hadn't been ducking the test, and he'd been competing for his country! "They said, 'Too bad, you're suspended,'" Wilson recalled.

Cochran had another message for the TAC officials and it was blunt. "I told them I was going to federal court if the suspension wasn't overturned," he said. "That would have been the appropriate place. We would have won, too, and we would have knocked them out of everything they were doing."

Within a few days, it was over. Marion's suspension was overturned by a two-to-one vote; a young woman attorney on the panel cast the negative vote, Wilson recalled with amazement. Marion was free to compete again.

One factor that worked in their favor, Wilson thought, was good timing. Track officials were beginning to realize just how unfair the system had become and to look for ways to correct it. After Marion's case was resolved, the drug-testing notification system was modified to include a phone number athletes can call to see if they are scheduled to report for testing.

Marion's mother was especially grateful for the kindness of Cochran and Wilson. "Do you know what Johnnie Cochran charged us?" she asked. "Nothing."

"My pay was seeing her win at the Mount Sac Relays the next year," Cochran said. "And now she's the greatest athlete in the world, the greatest woman athlete ever, I think. My greatest fulfillment will be seeing her win in Australia. I'll be there. I love that kid."

IN JUNE OF 1993 Marion won three events at the California state track and field championships: the 100, the long jump, and, in her final competition in high school, the 200. The result was an unprecedented nine championships in four years, and Bob McGuire, the manager of the meet, thought the feat should be recognized. McGuire stopped Marion as she came off the track, then called up into the stands to tell Dave Hurlburt, the public address announcer, what he had in mind.

"Ladies and gentlemen," Hurlburt announced, "in recognition of Marion Jones's achievement as the first person ever to win nine championships at the California state high school track meet, officials have asked her to take a victory lap."

McGuire pointed to the track and gave Marion a gentle shove. "She was a bit hesitant," he said. "It was more attention than she wanted. But she was a polite young person and if some adult asked her to do something, she'd do it."

A *victory* lap! Marion thought. Whoa!

As Marion went around the track, shyly waving as she ran, twelve thousand people rose to their feet, the cheers coming to a crescendo in one section of the stands after another as she passed by.

"The beauty of it is, it wasn't staged," said Dean Crowley. "It was just something that happened on the spur of the moment."

Marion's victory lap was the first one ever taken by an athlete at the state track meet, a meet that has been held since 1915.

# 3

The first college recruitment letter Marion received was from Arizona State. It arrived a week after she started her freshman year in high school.

Over the next four years the letters kept coming, and Marion's mother filled one box, then another, and then another until there were hundreds. About 70 percent, Marion estimated, were for track.

The reason for this is easy to understand. As Marion set national high school records and qualified for the Olympics, her reputation as a track prodigy spread around the country. Every state has its own basketball all-stars, however, and without a clock or a tape measure it's hard to compare them. So if Marion was one of a kind in track and field, she was part of the crowd in basketball.

"I got so many letters saying it would be in my worst interests if I played basketball in college," Marion said. "They said my future was in track."

But the schools that did their homework learned that the best way to capture Marion's attention was to agree to let her play both sports and to spend her junior year out of basketball while she tried out for the 1996 U.S. Olympic team. The University of North Carolina got a gold star on its homework assignment when it sent assistant track coach Curtis Frye and assistant basketball coach Fred Applin on the same recruiting visit.

Marion wanted to major in journalism and her mother began looking for colleges with a good record of graduating minority students who played varsity sports. They both agreed they were tired of California, and her mother had decided to move with Marion wherever she went. That's how they did it in Belize, she explained. Families stuck together. In the end the decision came down to three schools: Florida, Ohio State, and North Carolina. Even though she had never visited Gainesville, Marion was intrigued by the idea of Florida. Her mother preferred North Carolina.

"You'll be a Tar Heel," her mother told her one night as Marion was climbing the stairs to her room. "I just feel it in my heart."

"I'll be a Gator," Marion replied, still climbing.

"Marion, you're going to be a Tar Heel."

"Gator!"

"Tar Heel!"

"Gator!" Marion said, and she shut the door.

One visit to Chapel Hill and Marion became a Tar Heel.

"I met some professors, I met the basketball team, I walked around the campus, and I immediately had a good feeling," Marion said of her recruiting visit to the small, charming college town that has a passionate relationship with the university and its sports teams. "Having people walk by and say good morning, not even knowing you, I was blown back by that. Coming from California, where everybody kept to themselves, I knew this was where I wanted to go to school."

Marion was impressed by the highly rated journalism school and she liked the basketball players she met, particularly Sylvia Crawley, who acted as her "big sister" during her official visit. As she left for home she told Sylvia Hatchell, the North Carolina basketball coach, she'd be back.

MARION ENROLLED AT North Carolina in the fall of 1993 and her introduction to basketball there was gratifying. A solid Atlantic Coast Conference (ACC) team, the Tar Heel women had never matched the success of the men's team, which was coached by Dean Smith and reached its peak during Michael Jordan's playing days. They hadn't won the ACC tournament in Hatchell's seven years as coach, nor had they distinguished themselves in the NCAA tournament.

But the 1993–94 team had several excellent and experienced players returning, particularly in the front court, and they had high hopes of improving on a 23-7 season from the year before. One problem as practice began, though, was what to do with Marion.

Because she had always been one of the tallest girls on her high school team, Marion's coaches had tended to station her under the basket or out on the wing where she could cut to the hoop and score from close range. Al Walker, the coach at Rio Mesa, had been thinking of turning her into a playmaker, but then she transferred to Thousand Oaks where Michelle Palmisano, one of the best players in the state, was firmly entrenched at that position. So Marion never got much practice handling or passing the ball, and the result was that her main weakness as a basketball player lay in what was also her chief asset: her speed.

"The only problem I see with Marion," UCLA basketball coach Billie Moore once told Hatchell, rising to her feet to demonstrate, "is that sometimes she's here and the ball is back here." Which is to say, her ball-handling skills needed work.

But the more Hatchell contemplated her core of returning forwards and centers—Sylvia Crawley, Tonya Sampson, and Charlotte Smith—the more she was tempted by one daring idea: giving Marion the ball and the leadership of the team. After the second day of practice, the coach called her new recruit into her office.

"Marion, honey," Hatchell said, "I'm going to make you a point guard."

Marion was surprised and puzzled. "Coach Hatchell, are you sure you want to do that?" she said. This lady's crazy, she thought. But Hatchell remained steadfast. She was a self-described gym rat from Gastonia, North Carolina, who had been around basketball most of her life and had grown up a big fan of North Carolina basketball. Now in her dream job, she was pretty sure she knew what she was doing.

Marion worked on her dribbling and passing with Andrew Calder, a North Carolina assistant she took an instant liking to. After just a few weeks, she found herself thinking the experiment might work, and she wasn't alone.

"Marion has a focus on what she wants to do like no one I've ever seen," Hatchell said. "She lets no one and nothing interfere. And she's so coachable. She'd watch films, ask questions. Whatever you showed her, she would perfect it. She was like a sponge."

As she prepared for the season, Marion discovered there were some things she had to get used to. Hatchell was a proponent of weight training, and though Marion had done a little lifting in high school, she now began in earnest. Before long, she was pressing well over two hundred pounds and gaining the weight she needed to withstand the pounding of college basketball.

Then there were the Tar Heel women's unofficial practice sessions with men. Often the competition was from the junior varsity or some of the serious street players on campus, but occasionally some members of the North Carolina varsity, including future pros Jerry Stackhouse and Rasheed Wallace, would join in, and Marion would realize she wasn't in high school anymore.

"We'd be just as loud and intense as the guys," she said. "We'd be cursing like they were and if we would score in their face, we'd rub it in. Then they'd push us around a little bit. A lot of coaches say they don't like their women playing against the guys because it's too rough, but I think that helped us. We had some heated games."

But Marion discovered that the real joy of basketball at North Carolina was practicing with her teammates. No more high school girls looking for physical education credits. No more players who didn't have the skills or the dedication. Like Marion, the North Carolina players and their opponents had been recruited out of high school and had received scholarships. They were good.

"For the first time in my life," Marion said, "I was getting a chance to play against women who were as competitive as I was, who loved the game. We loved coming to practice. We loved scrimmaging. We loved drills. We'd finish practice at Carmichael Auditorium and go over to Woollen Gym and play pickup ball afterwards. I don't know if I'll ever find another bunch of players like that. It was wonderful."

COMING OFF THE BENCH in her first college game, Marion scored sixteen points and had eight steals in twenty-one minutes. By the fourth game she was the starting point guard, and whatever apprehensions there had been about her new position quickly disappeared.

"She understood the game," Tonya Sampson said. "It was just a matter of changing her attitude from being a shooter to a point guard, realizing she didn't have to score, just get the ball downcourt and pass it off. Once she got that in her head, we were home free."

Hatchell watched in satisfaction as all Marion's abilities were put to the test. It wasn't just offensively that Marion was making a difference at her new position, but defensively as well. With Marion playing back, other teams were afraid to pass the ball downcourt for a fast break for fear she would steal it and be gone. "When Marion gets the ball and is taking off down the floor," a referee told Hatchell, "I don't even try to keep up with her."

For Marion, it was like moving from Rio Mesa to Thousand Oaks all over again. Once more, she was reborn on the basketball court. She discovered she liked being in control, liked having the other players react as she set up the plays, and, most of all, liked being on a team with experienced players like Sylvia Crawley, Charlotte Smith, and Tonya Sampson. "It was crazy," she said. "I was a freshman, but they believed in me, they embraced me, and they said, 'You're going to be our point guard.'"

The only problem Marion had with her new role was one she had never had before: speaking up. A freshman was supposed to tell All-Americans like Tonya and Charlotte to try harder, react quicker, get their act together? No way. "She wasn't comfortable with it," Tonya said. "She said, 'I'd rather not talk, I'd rather show it on the court and you follow my lead.' I don't think she felt she had a right to talk."

But after the first few practices, when Marion found her teammates were not only listening to her but doing what she said, she lost her last vestiges of shyness. Surprised and honored by her teammates' respect, she began speaking up more and more often.

What particularly pleased Hatchell was how positive Marion was with her teammates. Rather than being critical when something went wrong or needed correcting, she always seemed to find a constructive way to get her point across. There were times, in fact, when the coaching staff felt the sting of Marion's positive ways with her teammates.

"Melissa, what kind of shot was *that*!" one of the coaches asked Melissa Johnson—who joined the team during Marion's senior year—after she had driven to the basket but failed to score. Marion responded by looking Melissa in the eye and, speaking up so everybody could hear, saying, "Good move, though."

"She immediately and simply negated the whole thing and quietly defied what the coach was saying," said Melissa, who realized Marion was standing up for her by accenting the *positive* aspect of what she had done. "There was never a question who her loyalties were with. They were to her teammates above all else."

THE PLAYERS RETURNING to North Carolina in the fall of 1993 were still upset about an embarrassing 74-54 loss to Tennessee in the NCAA tournament the previous spring. They had beaten themselves, they thought. With so many capable veterans, and the addition of their brilliant freshman, they craved redemption. After the first day of practice, Hatchell brought the team together in the center of the court where she had them grasp hands and say "National Champions!" They repeated the chant after each practice session the rest of the season.

With Tonya Sampson leading a balanced scoring attack, Charlotte Smith averaging more than nine rebounds per game, and Stephanie Lawrence hitting more than 40 percent of her three-point shots, North Carolina set school records that still stand for victories, winning percentage, assists, steals, blocked shots, and free-throw percentage. Marion averaged 14.1 points and 3.2 steals per game—school records for a freshman—and 4.1 rebounds and 2.8 assists.

The team lost only twice during the regular season, both times to Virginia, and the North Carolina players were delighted when they got another shot at the Cavaliers in the championship game of the ACC tournament. In the locker room before they took the court, Hatchell mentioned the two defeats and the fact that North Carolina had not won a conference championship since she had become coach. Then, looking around the room to gauge the response, Hatchell was stunned by what she saw.

"The intensity in Marion's eyes was like daggers going through my body," Hatchell said. "We hadn't even gone out to warm up yet and she had tears rolling down her face."

"When I saw her, I began to cry myself," Sylvia Crawley said. "It was contagious. We wanted to win so bad it hurt."

North Carolina beat Virginia 77-60, and raced through the NCAA tournament with only one close game, a 73-69 win over Vanderbilt that Charlotte Smith missed after being ejected from the previous game for fighting with an opposing player. Then, on April 3, in Richmond, Virginia, the Lady Tar Heels played in an

NCAA championship game that saw one of the greatest finishes in the history of basketball.

LOUISIANA TECH, LONG A basketball power among women's colleges, brought a 25-game winning streak to the Richmond Coliseum and, shortly after the game began, caught a big break. With less than six minutes gone, Marion was charged with her third foul and sat out the rest of the half. Floundering without its floor leader, the North Carolina team committed eight turnovers and shot poorly. It was saved only by the fact that Louisiana Tech couldn't find the basket either. At halftime, the score was tied.

Marion returned after the intermission, but the Lady Techsters took advantage of eleven consecutive scoreless possessions by North Carolina to take a 53-48 lead with 5:03 left. Charlotte Smith made a basket and a foul shot, and Sylvia Crawley scored on a turnaround jumper to tie the game; but, at the other end, Pam Thomas, a 5-3 guard who scored all fifteen of her points in the second half, hit a jump shot from the baseline to put Louisiana Tech up 59-57 with fifteen seconds to play.

With time running out, Marion brought the ball upcourt, saw Tonya Sampson in the key, and threw her a pass. Tonya pulled up for a ten-foot jump shot that would tie the game, and hit the front of the rim. The ball bounced free and a Louisiana Tech player got a hand on it, but Marion was there, too, forcing a stalemate. The whistle blew and everyone in the building looked at the clock, which read 00.7. North Carolina trailed by two points with seven-tenths of a second remaining.

For a moment, it appeared that the game was as good as over; although the ball should have belonged to North Carolina, the possession arrow favored Louisiana Tech. But officials quickly corrected the error and the teams went to the sidelines. Time for one play. Maybe.

Hatchell told Stephanie Lawrence, who would throw the ball inbounds, to try to get the ball to Sylvia Crawley under the basket. It was a play that had worked earlier in the game; Stephanie had been able to pass off to Sylvia because Louisiana Tech was preoccupied with Tonya, North Carolina's leading scorer. But don't gamble, Hatchell said. If she's not wide open, call another time-out.

But this time, the Lady Techsters were ready, sending three players down under the basket. "She was open for about a split second," Stephanie said of Sylvia, "but I didn't want to have it tipped."

Time-out.

As Hatchell watched the Louisiana Tech defense packed in under the basket, an ominous thought occurred to her. Even if North Carolina did get the ball in close, what chance was there of getting off a clean shot with so many players sitting there waiting? And could the referees really be expected to blow a whistle with a national championship on the line and less than a second remaining? They could knock us to the floor, Hatchell thought, and there would be no foul.

There was, she decided, only one option remaining. With so little hope of tying the game, North Carolina would simply have to try to win.

Tonya was instructed to head toward the basket and try to draw two defenders with her. Sylvia would set a screen for Charlotte Smith, who would make a move as if she, too, were trying to get underneath. But then Charlotte would step back behind the three-point line at the side of the court and take the pass from

Stephanie. The season would be in the hands of a post player used to getting her points in close, a player who had made only 26 percent of her three-point shots all season.

As soon as she made her move toward the basket, Tonya could see that the play had a chance. Louisiana Tech wasn't sending two players after her, it was sending three. Charlotte's going to be open, Tonya thought as the opposing players bumped her off course. Though she continued moving toward the basket for a possible rebound, she knew there would be no time and there was really only one thing she could do. Pray.

Watching the play develop as she guarded an opponent in the backcourt, Sylvia could see what Tonya could only sense: Charlotte was wide open.

Oh, God, Charlotte thought as she stepped back, took the inbounds pass from Stephanie, jumped, and let the ball fly.

And where was Marion at this critical moment? Where was the point guard, the team leader? Standing at the top of the key, hoping to decoy a defender, petrified.

"I couldn't even move," she said. "I'd never been in a situation where it was all riding on less than a second. All I could think was I was glad the play wasn't to me because my hands were frozen on my thighs. Every time they show the replay, it's that last second over and over again, and I always look at myself and shout, 'Move, Marion! Do something!' But it was wonderful. Quite wonderful."

Charlotte never saw the shot go in. Her teammates mobbed her as the buzzer sounded and North Carolina, with a 60-59 victory, was the NCAA champion.

The rest was a blur: an impromptu parade back on campus, a trip to the White House, a call and later a visit from Michael

Jordan. For the next two or three weeks, Marion and her roommate, Tonya Cooper, would turn to each other and grin. "Do you believe we're national champions?" they would say over and over again.

THE BEST EXAMPLE of Marion's impact on North Carolina basketball may be what happened when she sat out her junior year with an injury. In her championship freshman season, the team's record was 33-2. In her sophomore and senior years, it was 30-5 and 29-3 respectively. The season she missed, the Lady Tar Heels went 13-14.

But though North Carolina won the ACC tournament in each of her two subsequent seasons, it didn't advance beyond the Sweet Sixteen in the NCAA tournament. So Marion's accomplishments as an upperclassman took place on a smaller stage, and the truest connoisseurs of her talents were her teammates.

"I'm so jealous of you," Chanel Wright, who was a freshman the year Marion couldn't play, told Melissa Johnson after practice one day.

"Jealous?" Melissa said.

"You're getting this experience as a freshman," said Chanel, then a sophomore. "You have no idea what it was like last year. This is just so much fun!"

Melissa soon found out what she meant. It *was* fun. Basketball had never been like this, because neither of them had ever played with anyone like Marion.

"We had a standing joke about how as soon as the other team made a turnover, we'd just lob the ball upcourt for her," Melissa said. "It didn't matter where she was because she'd get to it. And everyone else was so at ease on the court they would loosen up and play that much better."

"There was a type of bond, a connection," said Jessica Gaspar, a guard who was a sophomore when Marion was a senior. Each knew the others' style, what moves they would make, and what they wanted to do on the court. "You put Marion on any team and that team's going to change. She held us together."

The best player Marion played with at North Carolina was Tracy Reid, who set the school's career scoring record and went on to play for the Charlotte Sting where she became the Women's National Basketball Association Rookie of the Year. An All-American in high school, Tracy had committed to the University of Florida, but she visited Chapel Hill the day of the parade celebrating the NCAA championship and was hooked.

She and Marion soon developed an uncanny rapport on the court. It seemed as if Tracy could almost sense when and where Marion would pass her the ball. One look from Marion and Tracy knew whether to stay away from the basket or cut underneath or run in a certain direction. And just as she got to where she was going, the ball would be there, too. It was astonishing, Tracy thought. After two practices, it seemed as if they had been playing together for years.

Marion's confidence in Tracy's skills was equally great. She was so much faster than the women guarding her, and she could jump so much higher, that at times it seemed as if they could run scoring plays at will. "We had some wonderful fast breaks," Marion said, grinning at the memory.

Soon the word on campus was that Tracy was North Carolina's most outstanding player and Marion the most valuable. Tracy had better statistics, but Marion was unquestionably the leader, the driving force. "She was the mother of the team," Melissa Johnson said.

Tracy and Marion were a fascinating pair off the court as well, once Tracy, who had barely said a word during her recruiting visit, revealed her true nature.

"Anything you want to hear?" Marion asked Tracy one night when she and Tonya Cooper were listening to music in their dorm room.

"How about this?" Tracy said, pulling a tape of 2 Live Crew out of her pocket and proceeding to sing every word of every song along with the rap group. Marion called Tracy "Hard Core" from that moment on. Soon, the two teammates were cutting loose in other ways, too: daring each other to run down the street outside their dorm in freezing weather wearing only shorts and a sports bra, cutting up at parties when they saw the fraternity and sorority members putting on self-important airs. They even devised a step routine, which they called the Hoop Phi dance.

"We were trying to get recognized on a campus where you still had the aura of Dean Smith and Michael Jordan and James Worthy," Marion said. "We wanted to find something to set ourselves apart and be noticed. The fraternities and sororities all had their step dances, and girls would be walking around with their noses in the air, so we did our own dance. Then everybody would pay attention to us and forget all about them. And if we would see one of our teammates across campus, we'd yell, 'Hoop phi!' and the person would shout back, 'You know!' It became our chant before games."

"That's the kind of bonding we had," Tracy said. "I miss that."

Tracy wasn't the only one who saw Marion loosen up and relax. In her freshman year, she and Tonya Cooper each saved up thirty-five dollars and went to one of Chapel Hill's scruffiest tattoo parlors, whose proprietor had a pierced tongue and eyelid, and tattoos all over his body.

"Let me just say he catered to an alternative crowd," said Marion, who chose a tattoo combining a flash of lightning and wings for the inside of her right ankle. People often ask her if it symbolizes speed, but she tells them it just looks cool. She returned to the tattoo parlor her junior year and had a frowning theatrical mask containing her initials applied to her left shoulder blade. "I told myself that one day I'd get the happy mask, too," she said, "but I haven't gotten around to it yet."

Marion's capacity for fun didn't fool those who knew her best, though.

"There was such an old soul about her, such wisdom," said Melissa Johnson. "You wondered if she could see herself the way other people saw her."

IF BASKETBALL WAS a source of great happiness for Marion in college, track and field was nothing but frustration. Arriving at track practice the spring of her freshman year, Marion was walking her bicycle down the stadium stairs when she misjudged the final step, fell, and twisted her ankle, which immediately began to swell. She soon recovered, but the pattern for her college track career was set. Marion never ran as fast or jumped as far in college as she had in high school. If she hadn't realized before coming to North Carolina that she was finally going to have to make a choice, she was learning in a hurry.

"If anything, I would have thought it would be the other way around," said Marion, to whom track had always come so easily.

"I would have thought track would be great and basketball would be pretty good. It was the exact opposite."

Marion's arrangement with North Carolina track coach Dennis Craddock was that she would get two weeks off after basketball, and, since the NCAA tournament run extended the season well into the spring, her time on the track was limited. The results were inevitable.

"I beat her! I beat her!" an opponent shouted after winning a sprint in Marion's sophomore year, and, indeed, Marion, who hadn't lost a race since her freshman year in high school, had to start getting used to it. At the NCAA championships in Boise, Idaho, her freshman year, she finished second in the long jump, sixth in the 200 and didn't make the finals of the 100.

"Here was this person who used to come down the runway and just power her way into the pit," said Doug Speck, the director of the Arcadia Invitational, as he saw her labor. "It looked to me like she could barely get off the ground."

How disappointing, thought John Capriotti, a Nike sporting goods executive who would later champion her future as a track star, noting the extra weight Marion had put on for basketball. On the other hand, he thought, to take second in the long jump with little practice and deficient technique certainly showed talent.

For Marion, not being able to perform at a high level for the first time in her life was frustrating. And the excitement of playing first-rate basketball, and of winning the NCAA championship as a freshman, made it even harder to concentrate on track. "My heart wasn't in it," she said. "I was going through the motions, and physically I didn't have enough time to practice, but subconsciously, I still expected to compete at a high level and when I couldn't do that, it was tough."

Craddock was equally disappointed. Though he had to honor the school's commitment to allow Marion to compete in two sports, he'd had designs on getting her on the track full time from the beginning.

"I was hoping that after a year or so she would see she wasn't going to be as good in basketball," he said. "After that first year, I knew it wasn't going to happen. If another great athlete came to me and said, 'I want to do both,' I'd have to think about it long and hard."

But Marion hadn't given up on track and she couldn't wait for her junior year to begin. It had been four years in the planning, arranged carefully in advance. She would take a year off from basketball, get back on the track in earnest and prepare for the Olympics. During the summer, Marion returned to California and moved in with her former coach, Elliott Mason, and his family. After just a few weeks of training, she could sense her sprinter's speed returning and her excitement beginning to mount.

She'd miss playing basketball, of course. She'd miss the magic she had made with Tracy Reid, but it was worth it to go to the Olympics. Which events should she try to qualify for—the 100, the 200, or the long jump? Maybe, she'd just enter all three.

In August Sylvia Hatchell called. The U.S. basketball team that was going to the World University Games needed a point guard, and they wanted Marion.

"Coach Hatchell," Marion said, "I'm training for track now. The Olympics. Remember?"

"It's up to you," Hatchell replied, "but I think this is a great opportunity for you to be a part of USA Basketball."

What the heck, Marion thought. She'd gotten her base work done in track. She was back in shape. A couple of weeks playing basketball wouldn't hurt. She flew to Colorado Springs where she joined the team, which had already begun practicing, and promptly broke her foot.

"We were scrimmaging and I dove for the ball that was going out of bounds and another player dove, too," Marion said. "I don't think she saw me, but she landed on my foot in a weird way."

Marion fractured the fifth metatarsal on the outside of her left foot, a small bone next to the stress fracture she had suffered her freshman year in high school. She flew to Chapel Hill where university surgeon Tim Taft put a screw in the bone and her foot in a cast. It would heal in plenty of time for the Olympics, he told her.

Marion did as she was told during her rehabilitation period. She swam, stretched, rode a stationary bike, and made constant visits to Taft's office where he monitored her progress. Good news, Taft told her in December after examining the latest X rays. The fracture had healed and she could start working out again. But take it easy at first, he said.

Marion began jogging and felt good; her speed for the sprints would be back in no time. Then, in January, she began thinking about the long jump. Just some nice, light, no-pressure drills so she could get the feel of being in the air again. What about that trampoline in the gym?

"I was just jumping up and down," she said, "kind of getting my balance, and I came down a little awkwardly and immediately felt a pop and heard a squeaking sound. I tried to jump again and I couldn't. It didn't hurt as much as it did the first time, but it hurt. I went to Dr. Taft right away, but I already knew I had re-broken it."

She had fractured the same bone in the same place. She had even bent the screw in her foot. In twenty years of performing that particular operation, Taft said, he had rarely seen a bent screw, and never in a fracture that had healed. He inserted a new, larger screw, along with bone marrow from Marion's hip to help the break heal faster.

Marion was devastated. The Olympics were out, and so was basketball. All she had to replace them were a permanent lump on her foot where the screw entered the bone and an abiding sense of helplessness. Everything that seemed important to her —her basketball teammates, her gold-medal dreams of twelve years standing—was gone. And, just as when she had broken her wrist in high school, the loss of sports was hard to bear.

"I couldn't play," Marion said of watching the basketball team struggle without her. "I couldn't practice. I couldn't be out there scrimmaging with them, hurting with them, going through all their ups and downs. My foot was in a cast, so I could hardly even walk around."

Feeling distant from her teammates and friends, Marion's depression grew. She lost interest in her classes, her grades suffered, and, just to top things off, Chapel Hill was hit with its worst winter in years, complete with a howling ice storm.

MARION WAS INTRODUCED to C. J. Hunter, the University of North Carolina's assistant track coach in charge of shot-putters and discus and javelin throwers, in the weight room.

"Hi," she said between lifts, as she worked on rehabilitating her broken foot.

"Hi," he said without breaking stride.

"You know, that C.J., he's a cute guy," one of Marion's track teammates said later. Marion smiled and thought nothing further about it.

GROWING UP IN Hyde Park, New York, C.J. was an avid baseball player, and he was crushed when he didn't make his high school team. A friend suggested he go out for track and he soon realized he had found his sport.

Surprisingly agile for a man who would eventually carry 320 pounds on a six one frame, C.J. threw the shot, discus, and javelin and became one of the top high school weight men in the country. He received a scholarship to Penn State, where he won a national collegiate title and a world ranking. C.J. placed seventh in the 1996 Olympics in Atlanta, and by 1997 he was consistently breaking seventy feet and moving up in the international standings.

Weight men and women are the foot soldiers of track and field. The spotlight doesn't seek them out as often as runners and jumpers, and the very nature of their events—short explosive exertions from people with large bodies off in a corner of the track—tends to make them seem less glamorous. That's what C.J. likes about the shot put.

"I don't want it to be like that," he said of the excitement Marion's events generate. "The last thing I want is visibility. I just want to throw far. It doesn't have anything to do with anybody watching me."

C.J.'s antic sense of humor, which is the delight of his close friends, almost never surfaces in public. Let people think what they want. It's fine with him. Nor does the idea of fame, and of tending to the publicity that feeds it, interest him. C.J. watches Marion do interview after interview, fresh and sparkling in each one, but he seldom submits to them himself. Even after placing in major track meets, when the medalists are expected to attend press conferences, his spot on the podium is often empty. "I don't care about that," he said. "Never have. All I need is a Notre Dame football game on television and I'm happy."

AS PART OF HIS coaching duties at North Carolina, C.J. would call prospective high school recruits from the track office in Carmichael Auditorium, which had been the school's only basketball arena before the Dean Smith Center was built in the mid-1980s. The women's team continued to play at Carmichael, however, and, after C.J. had made his calls to athletes in the East and Midwest in the late afternoon, he would take a break before turning to his West Coast list. To kill time, he would watch the Tar Heel women practice or play.

Soon, he became a big fan of the North Carolina women's basketball team, which had won the NCAA championship game two years earlier. This is quality stuff, he thought, as he watched Tracy Reid and the other North Carolina women. It's a shame he hadn't been exposed to it before. And he wondered how good the team would be if Marion weren't out for the season with an injury.

Early in 1996 Marion began going to track practice, although her leg was still in a cast and her workouts were confined to rehabilitation exercises. Bored and cranky because of her inactivity, she would occasionally speak to C.J., whom she found intelligent and analytical about track and field. After her ride to the airport fell through one day, C.J. volunteered to drive, and she discovered he also had the welcome quality of being able to make her laugh. She was never more relaxed, she realized, than when she was around him. He was making a hard time easier.

Marion and C.J. started going out to dinner and the movies. As they realized how much they enjoyed spending time together, they also realized they had a problem: Marion was a student and C.J. was a coach. University rules were clear that no personal relationships could be allowed.

"For a while we were dating on the DL," Marion said, "what they called the down low, hoping not too many people would see us."

But it wasn't reasonable to expect that one of the university's most celebrated female athletes would not be noticed in the company of someone as conspicuous as C.J. in a town the size of Chapel Hill. C.J. was soon called into Dennis Craddock's office and given an ultimatum: He could coach track or he could date Marion, but he couldn't do both. Within minutes, C.J. was out of a job.

Marion was concerned, finding it hard to believe that he could walk away from coaching so easily, that he could walk away from something he so obviously loved. He told her there would be more coaching opportunities, and that he figured he could train anywhere. "It's not a big deal," he said.

C.J. was honest with Marion about his wife, from whom he was separated, and two children in Colorado, and Marion was honest with herself. "I stepped back a little bit and thought about how it would affect me. But I wasn't thinking about marrying him. I thought, 'This is just a guy I'm dating and we're having fun together.'"

Months later, when her feelings had deepened, Marion had worked through her concerns about C.J.'s family, and about the fact that he was six and a half years older than she was.

By the fall of 1996 Marion was recovered from her injury and happily back playing basketball. If C.J. had been a casual fan of the Lady Tar Heels to that point, now he was a fanatic who never missed a home game and made a number of road trips. "I had no choice but to be interested then," C.J. said with a grin.

But C.J. found himself admiring more than just North Carolina's players. He enjoyed women's basketball as a whole, finding it more fundamentally sound than the men's game and lacking the display of egos he found so unappealing. In fact, he realized, he was becoming more appreciative of women's sports in general, particularly North Carolina's excellent women's soccer team, on which Mia Hamm and a number of the other U.S. national team players received their training. Why don't women get the credit they deserve? he wondered, as he watched the hours and the energy the North Carolina players devoted to their practice sessions. They work as hard as the men do. But even that thought seemed odd to him. Of course, they work as hard as men. Why wouldn't they? His conversion into a rabid women's sports fan was complete.

"Sometimes I come downstairs in the morning," Marion said, "and you know what C.J.'s watching? Tapes of my old college basketball games. He'll just sit there, rewinding them and playing them over again."

But if Marion's relationship with C.J. got him more interested in basketball, it had the opposite effect on her. Listening to him talk about working out, about traveling to track meets, and about preparing for the Olympics in Atlanta made her realize she had been ignoring her own track career, and that she truly missed it.

· · ·

ANOTHER PROBLEM DURING Marion's college years was her relationship with her mother, who lived in Carrboro, no more than ten minutes from her dorm, yet saw her daughter barely more often than if she had remained in California. "I wanted to be free," Marion said of the fact that she and her mother lived separate lives that converged only occasionally. "I wanted to do things on my own. I thought she was going to cramp my style when all she wanted was to see me grow up. I can understand that now."

Remembering how much she had missed her own mother, who had died when she was so young, Marion Toler rented a two-bedroom apartment so her daughter could visit when she tired of dorm life or wanted a home-cooked meal. "She never came," her mother said. "It broke me up."

Eventually a ritual developed. Marion would see her mother at basketball games, walk over and give her a kiss, exchange small talk for a moment, and then join her teammates. As much as six months might go by without a real conversation. Marion had never been one to talk about her feelings or to express her emotions, and even knowing that she was upsetting her mother couldn't change things. "But I knew by seeing her that she was fine," Marion said, "and I knew she knew that I loved her."

Marion's relationship with her coaches also began to deteriorate the year she was injured. Craddock didn't visit her when she broke her foot, and, when her grades suffered, Hatchell called her mother to say she was ordering her back to the dorm from the off-campus apartment, where she had moved. There is one thing you should know about Marion, her mother replied. No one orders her to do anything. But Hatchell didn't give up easily.

She told Marion she didn't think it was a good idea for her to be dating a man seven years older, with an ex-wife and two kids. Marion told her that C.J. made her happy, that he was making a difficult time much easier, and that she, her coach, of all people, should want her to be happy. It was a tense conversation, and it wouldn't be the last. The longer she remained at North Carolina, Marion began to realize, the more complicated things were going to become. The good times might be coming to an end.

MARION WENT TO THE 1996 Olympics after all —to watch C.J. compete in the shot put. But as pleasant as it was to have a rooting interest, the sight of Gail Devers, Gwen Torrence, and the other U.S. women sprinters could hardly escape her attention. Grinding her teeth and thinking, "Here's *another* Olympics," Marion began to wonder if she would ever return to the track. And once again, she realized how much she missed it.

"I didn't start playing organized basketball until I was in junior high," she said, "but I've been in track since I was seven years old. It was my first love."

Initially Marion kept her thoughts to herself, not even discussing them fully with C.J. "I had a feeling she might be thinking about coming back," he said. "But I wasn't clear on whether she was going to pick one sport over the other. I thought she might still try to do both. All I thought was that it was a huge decision and she needed to make it for herself."

Back on the basketball court in the fall, Marion maintained her silence. But as the season progressed, Hatchell began excitedly talking about the fine recruits who would be arriving to complement her the following year. North Carolina was sure to have an excellent season and might even win another national championship. Marion was due to graduate in the spring, but of course she would go to graduate school and use her remaining year of eligibility.

"She assumed I was going to come back and there was no reason for her not to," said Marion. Early in 1997 she decided she should tell the coach she was thinking of leaving. The two women disagree about what happened next.

Hatchell said she told Marion that she understood her reasons, that she agreed there was more money in track than in the new women's professional basketball leagues and that that was where her future was. She didn't try to talk her out of leaving, she said. The important thing was what was best for Marion.

Marion's memory of the conversation is different.

"She didn't take it well at all," she said. "She told me, 'You're not thinking this through correctly. You're going into this track and field thing blind. You haven't done this in a couple of years. A sure shot would be for you to come back to school, play basketball, and then go to the WNBA.'"

Marion suspected Hatchell thought C.J. was pressuring her, and finally she told her that nobody was making her do anything. This was what she wanted.

Marion and Hatchell did agree that she should say nothing to her teammates lest it prove a distraction, but almost immediately those closest to Marion began to suspect. Coming home late one night from a road game, Melissa Johnson, feeling particularly close to her friend, said, "Can you imagine if we never had a chance to play together again?" Marion remained silent and avoided eye contact. Melissa felt a chill.

"Marion, you're not looking at me," she said.

Marion told her she wasn't sure she would return and that she wouldn't make the decision until the end of the season.

Melissa was devastated. "I was convinced that this was it," she said. "She's going to become a famous track star when selfishly I just wanted her to stay."

Melissa returned to her dorm room and wrote a passionate e-mail message begging Marion not to leave. North Carolina would have such a great team the next season, she said. They could win a national championship. They were all counting on her. It wouldn't be the same without her. Later Melissa ruefully realized these were the same arguments Hatchell was using to try to make Marion feel guilty about leaving.

A year later, when Melissa herself decided to leave North Carolina and enroll at Harvard, where she had probably always belonged, she confided in Marion, who spent hours encouraging her to do what she thought was best for her. "She was a better friend to me," Melissa said, "than I was to her."

NORTH CAROLINA PLAYED SUPERBLY in Marion's final season, winning twenty-nine games, losing only three, and winning its third ACC tournament during her tenure. The team was seeded number one in the Eastern Regionals of the NCAA tournament, which meant it was rated one of the top four teams in the country. But things fell apart late in a tournament game against Michigan State when Jessica Gaspar took a pass from Marion, went up for a shot, and, as she came down, felt her knee give way as it if were held together with elastic. Jessica, whose passion and intensity meant so much to the team, suffered ligament damage that ended her season.

When she returned to the court to watch North Carolina win in overtime, it suddenly hit her. Her last game with Marion. The last pass she would ever take from her. The last memory on the court with her. "Only athletes who have been injured would un-derstand," said Jessica, who had also suspected what Marion was planning. "You don't realize you've been taking things for granted until they're gone."

Six days later, in an uncharacteristically flat and sloppy game, North Carolina was upset, 46-44, by George Washington. Marion scored eight points and had no assists. "I was so disappointed in myself," she said. "George Washington's defense was awesome—they shut me down—but all I could think was, My last college game and I'm going out like this."

ALL THAT WAS LEFT was to say good-bye.

The North Carolina women gathered in their spacious locker room for their annual end-of-the-season meeting, where Hatch-ell spoke and some bookkeeping matters were discussed. As the session dragged on, Melissa Johnson kept looking at Marion, whose face was expressionless. Finally the meeting began to break up and Melissa grew excited.

She's changed her mind, she thought. She not going to go after all. Let's get out of here.

But then Hatchell said, "Wait, Marion has something to say."

Marion said all the right things. Her time at North Carolina had been special. The women on the team were like her sisters. The times they'd had together had been wonderful. They would always have a special place in her heart. But it was time for her to move on, to return to the track and chase her dreams. She would be rooting for them next season.

There was something odd about Marion's farewell, though. She was looking up at the ceiling, down at the floor, around the room, everywhere except at her audience. Finally she caught a glimpse of Tracy Reid, old Hard Core herself, in tears.

Tracy had heard the rumors about Marion leaving but had refused to discuss them with her for fear they might be true. Unable to look at Marion, she put her head down and began quietly to cry. Soon others were crying, including Marion. "Marion's a strong person, but once we made eye contact, it was all over," Tracy said.

"Tracy will show emotion on the court," Marion said, "but when it comes to sentimental feelings, that's not her at all. So when she started crying, I knew I wasn't going to make it."

The true test of her teammates' affection came during the next few minutes when, one at a time, they came up to hug her, to tell her they were behind her, and to wish her luck.

THE ONLY TIME Marion felt a twinge of regret over not returning to school for one final basketball season came as the season was ending. In her three years of competition, she had never played Tennessee, the top team in the country, and now here were her friends playing the Volunteers in the 1998 Sweet Sixteen at Vanderbilt. The night before the game, she sent a fax wishing them good luck and, to each player on the team, a red rose.

Although Tennessee came into the game having beaten its previous tournament opponents by an average of more than thirty-one points, North Carolina led by twelve late in the game. Finally, however, Tennessee's superiority asserted itself and Pat Summitt's team won the game 76-70 and, shortly thereafter, its third consecutive national championship.

"Tennessee, Tennessee, that's all I heard all year long," said

Tracy Reid, who was named an All-American and the ACC Player of the Year. "And then when we finally got to play them and I could see we were going to lose, do you know what I was thinking? I was thinking if only Marion were here. If we only had Marion."

(Clockwise from top right) Marion at home in Los Angeles, age two; Marion at age ten, on the soccer team her mother and brother coached; Marion's little league team, age ten; Marion in her Dodgers T-ball uniform, age seven.

*(Clockwise from top right)
Marion at the 1991 U.S. Track
and Field Championships, age
fifteen; Marion on her way to
finishing sixth in the 100 meters
at the 1992 U.S. Olympic Trials,
age sixteen; Marion's Olympic
Trials credentials; Marion and
her mother at her final California
state championship meet.*

*Marion's defensive play helped her become the 1997 ACC Tournament MVP and helped the Tar Heels win the tournament championship.*

(Clockwise from top right) Marion and her teammates—Laquanda Dawkins, Sheneika Walker, Tonya Cooper, Tracy Reid, Nicole Walker, and Tanya Sampson —meet the other MJ, Michael Jordan, at the 1995 NCAA Tournament; With Jessica Gaspar and Tracy Reid after Marion's final game, 1997; With best friend Melissa Johnson; Marion announces the end of her UNC basketball career, 1997.

(Top) Marion at the 1997 U.S.A. Track and Field Championships; (Bottom) Marion on her way to victory in the 100 meters at the 1997 World Championships in Athens.

*(Clockwise from top right) A light moment at the 1998 U.S.A. Track and Field Championships; Conferring with Jackie Joyner-Kersee; Marion winning the 100 meters at the 1998 Goodwill Games; A quiet moment before the Goodwill Games victory.*

# 4

When Marion returned to the track in April 1997, a month before graduating from North Carolina, she had no idea what the future would hold. But it didn't take her long to realize what the present would consist of: pain.

"It was hell," she said of how she felt after sprinting, jogging, stretching, and doing her cardiovascular exercises. Under C.J.'s direction, she also began an intense weight program very different from her basketball workouts, which had sometimes degenerated into nothing more strenuous than dancing and singing with Tracy Reid.

"I was in great shape for basketball," Marion said. "I could run up and down the court all day. But doing drills and running around the track made me use muscles I hadn't used in four years." Hip-flexor muscles, shoulder muscles, calf muscles, they all hurt. Marion would come home from practice to the small apartment in Chapel Hill she shared with C.J., and he would ice down her legs and lower back while she just lay there, thinking she was too young to feel so old.

One problem was her weight—165 pounds—which was fine for basketball but at least 15 pounds more than she carries today. It was like trying to run down the track with a fully packed suitcase on her back. But Marion worked out in earnest and within about a month, she could sense a change.

"All of a sudden, I was able to do sprint workouts I couldn't have done two weeks earlier," she said. "I was doing things I hadn't been able to do since high school. It was like my body was saying, Where have you *been*?" Soon, the extra weight was gone, and her body was becoming elegantly muscled through her stomach, shoulders, and legs.

Early on, Marion decided not to work out on the North Carolina track. Dennis Craddock had not been pleased by her decision to give up her final season of eligibility any more than Sylvia Hatchell had, and C.J.'s response to Craddock's ultimatum did not make him popular in the athletic department, either. So Marion began to work out at Paul Derr Field on the campus of North Carolina State, the Tar Heels' arch rivals.

"There was just too much tension with the coaches at Carolina," Marion said. "I felt it would be better for everybody if I got away." What Marion did not know was that there was already a group of world-class athletes working out at Paul Derr, and that they had the one thing she lacked: a coach.

TREVOR GRAHAM LEFT his native Jamaica when he was fourteen years old, moved with his family to Long Island, and later attended St. Augustine's College in Raleigh, where he quickly became a star, winning the NCAA Division II quarter-mile championship in 1987.

The following year Trevor wanted to compete in the Olympics

in Seoul, but knowing he had little chance of making a U.S. team that boasted a number of world-class 400-meter runners, he went back to Jamaica where he thought his record would earn him a warm welcome. But Jamaican track officials not only didn't know who he was, they didn't seem particularly interested in finding out. You're not Jamaican, you're American, they told Trevor, who had to send for his birth certificate to prove them wrong. And when he did show up at the Jamaican Olympic trials, he found he hadn't even been assigned a number.

"They just gave me an outside lane, the worst one, and told me to go out and run," Trevor said. "I guess they didn't think I would make the team." He did, though, and he won a silver medal at Seoul in 1988 as part of the Jamaican $4\times400$-meter relay team, finishing behind a U.S. team that set a world record.

Hoping to continue his running career, Trevor took a job as assistant track coach at Kansas State where he impressed the head coach, John Capriotti, as extremely conscientious. "Trevor would spend all day on the track, coaching anybody who wanted to get better," said Capriotti, who later became Nike's sports marketing director for running.

But as much as he enjoyed teaching proper running techniques, Trevor was dissatisfied with what he was learning. His own coaches had done little more than set up a schedule of drills —so many sprints per day, so much distance work, so many starts out of the blocks—and Trevor knew there had to be more to it than that. There had to be someone with more technical knowledge, someone who could challenge his own theories about running.

Trevor began discussing his problem with a Kansas State physiology professor, asking him how the body processes oxygen during intense physical activity, how the various acids and chemicals that occur naturally affect performance, and how muscle mass and lung capacity factor into running faster. "You should be studying physiology if you want to know these things," the professor told Trevor. And soon he was.

"I learned about all the systems in the body," Trevor said, "and about physics and gravity. What I wanted to know was things like how long can you run at a certain tempo? What will happen to your body if it keeps going at a high rate of speed? Will it shut down? Will you just pass out? These were the things I had to know."

In 1991 Trevor moved back to Raleigh, took a job as a security officer at Glaxo Wellcome, a large pharmaceutical manufacturer, and spent his evenings at the St. Augustine's track, searching for athletes who needed a coach. He began with his wife.

Ann Graham was ranked seventh in the United States among 400-meter hurdlers. The plan was to work her way up to the top three, which would earn her a trip to the 1992 Olympics in Barcelona, and to recruit other athletes for her coach and husband. Ann worked hard, but with a three-year-old at home, and with a full-time job teaching school, her training time was limited. At the Olympic trials in New Orleans, she made it to the semifinals of the hurdles and was eliminated.

"I was hoping she would make the team, for her sake," Trevor says, "but it would help me, too. I'll admit it. I was very disappointed."

Little by little, though, Trevor began to develop a reputation as a coach whose methods worked. Chief among those he helped in the beginning was Antonio Pettigrew, a world-class quarter-miler he had met at St. Augustine's with whom he instantly formed a bond. Pettigrew's times improved and soon he was preparing for the World Championships. By the time Trevor moved his base of operations to Paul Derr Field, he was working with more than a dozen athletes, but since his fees were modest, he had to keep working at Glaxo Wellcome. Then he met Marion and things changed.

Trevor had seen Marion run while she was in high school and had seen her play basketball on television, and he also knew C.J., who had worked briefly at St. Augustine's after leaving North Carolina. As Marion warmed up and the two men chatted, Trevor never took his eyes off her.

"Just watching her that first day, I could see how powerful she was," Trevor said. "She was just so much more explosive than any woman I've seen since Florence Griffith Joyner. Her technique needed work and she was a little overweight from basketball, but the skills she had, the ability and the competitiveness, you can't teach them."

This was a common observation. Even back in high school, Marion's coaches remarked that coaching sometimes seemed beside the point. "It was hard to get too technical with her, because she ran like the wind," said Art Green, her coach at Thousand Oaks High School. "My coaching tended to be along the lines of, 'Hey, that's great. You're looking real good today.' I could never go wrong with that."

C.J. saw Trevor watching Marion practice and asked if he had any suggestions. One or two, Trevor replied, and he mentioned the "drive phase" he taught sprinters to use as they were coming out of the starting blocks. Marion was popping up at the start, he said, which wasted time. She should be staying low, keeping her head down.

"Why don't you show her?" C.J. said, and soon Trevor was moving Marion's blocks back a bit, showing her how to stay down, and suggesting she swing her arms a little more loosely. To Marion, who realized she was tensing up when she ran, the advice made a difference in a matter of seconds. "Everything just clicked," she said.

"She was picking up everything I taught her immediately," Trevor said. "It was like she knew all along and was just waiting for someone to tell her to do it."

None of this was lost on C.J., who was timing Marion's starts with a stopwatch. He reached out, tapped Trevor on the shoulder and said, "You coach her."

And he has ever since.

"It was all very up in the air," said Marion of her thoughts until that moment. "I needed to be in the hands of somebody who knew what he was doing. I thought maybe I'd have to go back to California and find a coach."

"Trevor has the right temperament for Marion, and his work ethic is in her," said John Capriotti. "I think he deserves a lot of the credit for what's happened."

Trevor's temperament is one of easy affability and generous smiles. At times he seems more Marion's friend or teammate than her coach, and soon Marion's faith in him was all but absolute as she turned her workout schedule over to him with only one request: Surprise her. "He tries to change it up on me so I can't guess what I'm going to do," she said. "I don't really like to know what I have to do the next day because I'll think about it all night. We both want it to be spontaneous."

So one day Trevor will emphasize sprint work and the next day he will have Marion run longer distances. At other times, the long jump may be emphasized, or starting out of the blocks. "It's funny," Trevor said, "but we never argue. She never even asks questions: 'Should we change this? Why are we doing that?' She just seems to trust me. We were both looking for each other, I guess."

For Marion, working with Trevor was like going back to school. He broke running down into its component parts in a way she had never considered before.

Drive phase, transition, body angle, chin position, arm swing, cycling motion, keeping her feet under her body, not leaning forward at the finish line—who knew there was so much to learn? "We'd be on the track four or five hours because Trevor was teaching me so slowly," Marion said. "I could run fast, but I didn't have any type of technique."

Head down, body low to the ground, arms relaxed, Trevor would say over and over again. That's the drive phase, the way you create force on the track. Pull up slowly into the full running position. That's transition. Pretend there's a rubber band holding you back and then suddenly it's let go. Or think of a car that you push, push, push, until suddenly it's running on its own.

Chin low, body leaning just slightly forward, arms pumping like you're beating a drum, legs underneath, not flailing out behind. Imagine you're riding a bicycle. Don't lean into the tape at the finish line. It's a natural instinct, but it slows you down by pushing your legs out behind your body. And don't look at the clock, either. It will only make you want to lean. These are not things Marion thinks about during a race, but during training it sometimes seems as if they are all she thinks about. And after a while, she could sense an important change. Proper technique became a matter of instinct, not thought.

Stopping by after his shot put workouts, C.J. was also fascinated by what Trevor was teaching. There was nothing he could teach her about running, he thought, but there was plenty he could learn. And besides, it was a pleasure to watch somebody so good at what he does.

"We'll be in an airport," Marion said with a grin, "and C.J. will say, 'Trevor, is she supposed to cycle like this?' And there will be this 320-pound man practicing his sprint technique."

The drills did wonders for Marion's time and confidence, and later, when she began running in Europe, the talk among the athletes was not just about her speed, but about her technique as well. "Marion Jones," said British sprint champion Linford Christie, summing up a common wisdom that tickled her to no end, "runs like a man."

Not long after he began working with Marion, Trevor realized that her time away from serious competition would not present an insurmountable challenge in preparing for the 1997 track season that was already under way. Her weight had come down nicely, her ability to learn quickly made for a steadily improving technique, and, within just a few weeks, Trevor was clocking her at 11.19 in the 100 meters. It would not be long, he thought, before she was breaking the eleven-second barrier for the first time and joining the world's elite women sprinters. But more than that, Trevor thought, Marion might have an advantage over the others. Her years playing basketball may actually have helped.

"She was very explosive," he said. "She could jump higher, and I think basketball taught her to be more aggressive than when she was younger. She had to learn how to compete in track again because basketball is a group thing and in track it's all up to you. You don't practice so the team can win. You do it so you can win.

She had to learn all over again that she could only rely on herself."

Marion thought her time off the track had provided another benefit, too. Getting away had kept her legs, and her love for the sport, fresh. "I see some of the people I went to high school with who ran track in college and now they're burned out," she said. "They competed in age group, junior high, high school, and all through college. By the time they were ready to run track for a living, they were physically and mentally exhausted."

Marion also had another motivation, because in Trevor she had acquired not just a coach but a set of teammates as well. The other athletes he worked with gave her just the support she needed, especially in her discouraging early days back on the track. "Stick with it, stick with it," Antonio Pettigrew would tell her. Later, when Chandra Sturrup, a sprint champion and long jumper from the Bahamas, arrived, she had not only a friend but also a practice partner who tests her limits every day and is tested herself in return.

"I don't think of her as a competitor when we're practicing," said Chandra of what it's like to work out on a daily basis with a superior athlete. "So it's not frustrating. But I have to try to stand up to the challenge, to try to learn from her and get better."

Chandra was not the only one who felt that way. "She kind of turned the whole group around," Trevor said of Marion's presence. "They all began thinking more professionally. It's like, 'If I do what Trevor says and think like Marion thinks, I can make it, too.'"

ON APRIL 19, 1997, Marion returned to competition at the Florida Invitational in Gainesville where her performances, 11.37 in the 100 and 21-8 in the long jump, were nothing special. She was thrilled. "To have only been training for a few weeks, it made me so excited," she said. "If I ran 11.37 now, people would say, 'What's wrong?' But I was just so happy."

The news kept getting better. At the Carolina Invitational in Chapel Hill on May 10, Marion ran 11.19, a dramatic improvement that made her feel euphoric. The small amount of doubt still remaining was gone now. Any lingering concern that she had made the wrong decision had disappeared. In high school, Marion had always viewed any track she stepped on as her turf. But for four long years, she had no longer had that feeling, and now it was back.

"I needed to prove to myself that I still had it," she said, "and when I started running fast again, I thought, You did the right thing, Marion. You did good this time."

The big breakthrough came at the Tennessee Invitational on May 24 in Knoxville where, with help from the wind, Marion ran the 100 in 10.98.

"Trevor and C.J. and I were going crazy," Marion said. "Under eleven seconds for the first time in my life, who cares if it's wind-aided? We knew that bigger things were going to happen than we initially had thought. I knew I was ready to do something special."

The only bit of unpleasantness during these early months occurred toward the end of April when Marion discovered that though she might be on the verge of leaving North Carolina, the university was not through with her.

As one of the world's leading shot-putters, C.J. had a deal with Nike that provided equipment, a modest training stipend, and performance bonuses. Aside from what he could win on tour, and a little financial assistance from C.J.'s agent, Charlie Wells, it was really the only money he and Marion had, and it made them fiercely loyal to the Beaverton, Oregon, company when other firms came calling after she became a hot commodity on the international sporting-goods market.

Marion and C.J. weren't starving, to be sure, but they weren't eating out much, either. Once, when their phone line went down and they didn't have enough money to turn it back on immediately, they had to use the pay phone at the Hardee's down the street. "Those are the type of things that brought us together even more," Marion said. "We were still happy."

C.J. had discussed Marion's comeback with John Capriotti of Nike, who invited her to run on a relay team at the Penn Relays, one of the most historic meets in the country. But when she arrived, Capriotti had some bad news. Dennis Craddock had called to say that Marion was still eligible at North Carolina, and, since the university was paying for her scholarship, she could not wear the colors of a sporting-goods company while she was in school.

Craddock was wrong on two counts. Marion's scholarship was for basketball, and the season was over, and NCAA rules and practices accommodate seniors who are no longer competing and are close to graduation. College football and basketball players, for instance, are free to sign with professional teams and still finish school once they are through playing. Unless North Carolina chose unilaterally to throw her out of school, hardly a likely scenario, the few months left on Marion's scholarship were not in jeopardy.

But the damage was done. Still upset that Marion hadn't abandoned basketball for track, Craddock had given her a going-away present, one that permanently damaged whatever feeling she still had for the sport at her alma mater.

"But I told him I was leaving," Marion protested. "I haven't run for North Carolina in two years. He knows I'm not coming back."

"Marion, it's not worth it," Capriotti said. "People might think we enticed you to run. Look at it this way. If this is the worst thing that ever happens to you, you're going to have a great career."

Marion withdrew from the relay and competed unattached in the long jump instead, finishing second. Capriotti, watching closely, was impressed. "I wanted to see how her body looked," said the man who had been so disappointed when he had seen her long jump in the NCAA championships three years earlier. "It was a total transformation. I thought, 'Ooo, boy, I'll die on the sword for this one.'"

But when Capriotti recommended signing Marion to a Nike contract, his superior, Mark Bossardet, turned him down. It was too soon, Bossardet said. There was plenty of time to see what she was capable of first.

Two months later, Capriotti and Bossardet had another conversation.

"Sign her," Bossardet said.

"You understand the price just went up, don't you?"

"I understand. Don't leave here without a deal."

The discussion took place in Indianapolis where Marion had just shaken the world of track and field to its roots.

IF MARION STILL HAD any doubts about her progress, her coach did not. Low key and cautious by nature, Trevor was not given to inflated rhetoric or extravagant predictions. So when a reporter from *USA Today* called after the Tennessee Invitational to ask how fast he thought Marion might run during her first year back, Trevor gave him an honest answer: 10.76. There was silence at the other end of the line.

"Ten seventy-six?" the reporter finally said. "Are you sure?"

"I'm sure," Trevor said.

"Can I print it?"

"Go ahead and print it, because she's going to do it."

The reporter saved the story until the eve of the U.S. Nationals in Indianapolis in June where it caused a sensation. Ten seventy-six! The world *record* had been 10.76 until Florence Griffith Joyner broke it in 1988. Only three women in history—Florence, Merlene Ottey, and Evelyn Ashford—had ever run that fast. Bombarded by questions about the prediction before the meet, Marion took them in stride. Trevor was just saying what he thought, she told reporters. "I did tell him that if he's ever going to make predictions again to let me know first, though," she said.

Trevor's prediction had a profound effect. When Marion and the other runners came onto the track for the first heat of the 100, everything seemed to stop. The crowd grew silent as they crouched in their blocks, and Marion could feel her mind racing. Her first competition in years against some of the best runners in the world. Her first step in so long into the national spotlight. Her first chance to see how her training would hold up over several days. Her first chance to prove she was not just another high school phenom who was past her prime.

The gun went off.

Marion's mechanics as she raced down the track were smooth, flawless, almost beautiful, Trevor thought. All the practice, all the coaching, all the planning was paying off as she seemed to gain speed with every step. The fact that Marion had cut her hair into a short, no-frills natural before the meet only seemed to add to the force and energy she exuded. Her time, 10.98, was the fastest of the year and bettered her five-year-old personal best by .16 seconds. It was only the first heat. There were two more races to go, but she was on her way.

"If you had touched me, I wouldn't have felt anything," she said. "But I really didn't have a chance to get excited or enjoy the moment. I just wanted to get on to the next round." Marion won the semifinals later in the day in 10.92 and people were buzzing about her acceleration and finishing kick. You have a good shot to win this thing, she told herself.

The next day, Marion was disappointed when, with the runners already on the track, Gail Devers withdrew from the final with a calf injury. Running against the country's best was one thing, but facing a two-time Olympic champion was another. Oh, well, she thought, this was one disappointment she was just going to have to move past.

She moved past everybody else, too. Surprised at how powerful she felt, and how well her technique was holding up through each subsequent race, Marion ran 10.97 into a headwind. Less than three months after she had returned to the track, she was a national champion.

Nobody in Indianapolis seemed to know quite what to make of the speed of Marion's ascent. "We all knew she was fast," said Inger Miller, who finished third, just behind Chryste Gaines and several yards behind Marion. "But we also knew it takes years to reach a high level. Everyone was shocked how quickly she hit those times."

And for once in her life, Marion didn't seem to know what to say, either. Handed the public-address microphone on the field,

Marion thanked the crowd and said how excited she was because she had only been back on the track for a few months. Then she saw Chryste and Inger hanging their hands and kicking at the dirt as if they were thinking, *We've* been doing it twenty years.

"I hope nobody took it the wrong way," Marion said. "It wasn't meant to put anybody down."

The next day, across the country in Mission Viejo, California, Al Joyner put down the paper, turned to his wife and said, "Honey, Marion Jones just did what you did. Every round in the nationals under eleven seconds."

"I was wondering what happened to her," Florence Griffith Joyner said.

THE ONLY PERSON Marion ever felt nervous about competing against was Jackie Joyner-Kersee. Jackie was one of the women whose accomplishments had transfixed her when she was young, and though competing against Evelyn Ashford and Gwen Torrence as a fifteen-year-old had not fazed her much, she was older now and not quite so blasé. Her accustomed confidence gave way to butterflies when she met Jackie, the U.S. long jump champion for seven consecutive years, at Indianapolis.

Once the competition began, however, Marion was pleased to see her competitive instincts take over and her nervousness disappear. On her first jump, she took the lead at 22-3¾, two inches beyond her personal best. Her landings were awkward—with so little time to prepare, almost all of her practice sessions had been devoted to the sprints—but again her natural talent saw her through.

Marion's lead held up through the first three rounds, when the field was cut and the jumpers competed in reverse order of the standings. This gave her the advantage of jumping last, and when Jackie fouled on her fourth jump, Marion passed. But on Jackie's fifth try, she jumped 22-8 to take the lead, and once again Marion felt a bit unnerved by the circumstances.

She was jumping against an idol, one of the greatest athletes in history, for the national championship. She would have to jump more than half a foot farther than her personal best at the beginning of the day to win. Go for it, she told herself. You've made the team for the World Championships. You have nothing to lose so leave it all out there. If you foul, you foul.

She jumped 22-9 and won by an inch.

The next thing she knew, Jackie was hugging her and, shortly thereafter, fending off embarrassing questions about passing the torch and hailing her as a coming star. What a wonderful person, Marion thought. There was no way she would be able to handle things this well when she was nearing the end of her career. Jackie, who soon became Marion's friend and confidante, was equally charmed by the newcomer. "There are so many of us who do great things on the athletic field and we just forget other people exist," Jackie told a reporter. "And that's sad. Even though she belongs on the pedestal, she doesn't act like she owns the pedestal."

Watching the tape of her winning jump later, Marion had to laugh. She may have shown some of the worst technique ever. Everything was just wrong. Her approach, her takeoff, her form in the air, her landing. But she had won. She had gotten off the best jump in the world of the year to date. Just imagine what she could do when she had some time to practice and to learn.

Summing up the 1997 U.S. Nationals, *Track & Field News* declared, "Marion's trip to Hoosierland was like an earthquake shaking Los Angeles, Jones's hometown. In an instant, the U.S. track world remembered a recently slumbering giantess." The words on the magazine's cover, superimposed over Marion's picture, put it more simply:

"She's Back!"

MARION'S EXPLOITS IN Indianapolis made her the subject of intense curiosity among the directors of the big European meets, who wanted to see the American phenom for themselves. They offered appearance money to lure her; not a lot, a few thousand dollars a meet and some bonuses for winning and running good times. A gold medal at the World Championships in Athens in August would be worth fifty thousand dollars, but who had time to think about that now? Charlie Wells told Marion to pack.

Marion quickly learned that running in Europe was not easy: She dealt with jet lag, hotel rooms, the language barrier, endless press conferences with reporters looking for news to pass on to fans who actually cared about the sport. C.J.'s experience at international meets helped, but there was one thing he could not help Marion with: the competition. The biggest meets drew the top athletes in the world. This was where they made their living and this was where they were ready to perform at their best, every week.

Marion's tour began with victories in the 100 at meets in Turin, which had a relaxed small-town atmosphere and drew only a few thousand people, and Zagreb, which was equally laid back. Though her times were nothing special in these early meets, it felt good to get her feet wet. Then she went to Lausanne, where she could feel the excitement level mount. The buildup was tremendous; many of the questions at the pre–meet press conference were directed to her, the crowd was loud and enthusiastic, and she was finally going to get her chance to run against Gail Devers.

Marion ran 10.90, a personal best. She also ignored everything she had learned about technique and lost. She didn't lose because she wasn't ready, Trevor scolded her. She lost because she forgot everything they had been working on. Stick to the plan, he said. Don't go back to running the way you used to. Upset, Marion knew Trevor was right and that she would have won if she had maintained her technique. So much to learn, she thought. So much to remember.

Two days later in Oslo, Marion got another chance against Gail. Although her time, 11.06, was slower, at last she beat the two-time Olympic champion. Pleased that she had paid attention to form this time—head down, drive phase, transition—Trevor considered it one of her most significant victories to date.

A week and a half before the World Championships, Marion went to Monaco. It was the first time she had really been able to take a deep breath since Indianapolis, and the sun, the sea, and the swimming seemed to drain all the tension away. When Charlie Wells rented a boat so the entire party could go out into the Mediterranean, she thought she was in heaven.

Even the training sessions seemed to relax her. With no meets on the schedule before Athens, she spent her time going over the basics again, refining her technique, and getting in some drills in the long jump, which she had entered in addition to the 100 and the 4×100 relay. At least nobody could accuse her of not jumping into her first World Championships with both feet.

. . .

ATHENS WAS HOT, noisy, and crowded and Marion felt slightly overwhelmed. Here she was at the World Championships. Center stage. The big time. It's all here, she thought. The opportunity for great success or failure lay right out in front of her. She would either live up to her promise and early success, the years of expectations heaped upon her, or she would leave Athens chastened.

Fortunately there were two early heats of the 100 to occupy her attention, and when she ran 11.03 in the morning and 10.96 in the evening, the smile on Trevor's face reinforced her own confidence. The only disconcerting notes were a 10.90 clocking by Zhanna Pintusevich of Ukraine—blazing fast for an early heat—and the sound of the starter's gun, which was unlike anything Marion had ever heard before. Instead of the sharp report of a bullet, it seemed more like an echo, a computer-generated echo that could be hard to pick up if she wasn't paying attention. Many runners grunt as they come up out of the blocks, she reminded herself. She would have to keep her wits about her.

The semifinals the next day had the feeling of a championship race. Marion found herself matched against Merlene Ottey, the great Jamaican sprinter, who, at the age of thirty-seven, was still among the best runners in the world. Invigorated by the challenge, Marion ran fast, 10.94, and won the heat. Had she run *too* fast? she wondered when she saw that Merlene had come in second at a leisurely 11.08. Zhanna Pintusevich, who ran 11.10 in her semifinal, obviously hadn't extended herself, either. With the final coming up in just over an hour, the question was whether Marion had saved enough.

This has to be the longest tunnel in the world, Marion thought after she left the warm-up track, walked over to the stadium, and disappeared down into the dungeonlike entrance to the infield. She wondered if they had put it there just so the runners would have plenty of time to think and get nervous. She came out into the heat of the infield, saw the huge crowd in the stands, picked her way through the dozens of people milling around, and approached the starting blocks.

Merlene Ottey's race was over before it began. A veteran of so many competitions, she didn't hear the second sound from the starter's gun signaling a false start and raced half the length of the track before pulling up. Giving herself all the time she dared to get her wind back, Merlene seemed to take forever walking back to the blocks, and though Marion knew she'd have done the same thing, she couldn't bear to watch. She wanted to run so badly that finally she just turned around, closed her eyes, and tried to regroup. She eased her legs into place and her feet against the blocks, carefully placed her long fingers along the starting line, took one last look down the track, blew out a lungful of air, and slowly, slowly, lowered her head and waited for the gun.

Marion got out of the blocks perfectly. She felt smooth and strong through her drive phase, gradually raising her head and and her torso as her arms pumped forward, always forward. She came up and stretched out to her full, long stride exactly as she had practiced so many times. Good, she thought. Real good. And then, at about sixty meters, she felt the oddest sensation.

She was alone.

There was nobody around her, nobody near her. The others had been there next to her, breathing and straining, and then they were gone. Chaos behind her, but perfect order—a line, a tape, an unbroken stretch of track—in front. Could she possibly be beating everybody by this much?

Without meaning to, without really realizing it, she relaxed slightly until, about twenty-five meters before the end, she felt somebody behind her, closing ground fast. She tried to run faster, straining forward as Zhanna Pintusevich made her move.

Shifting back to top speed after letting up is never easy and Marion's technique deserted her during the final fifteen meters. It was as if she were back in high school again. Get to the finish line, she told herself. Just get there. Don't worry about how.

As she crossed the line, Marion thought she had won. She'd leaned across first, she was sure of it. And then she saw the mass of photographers running up the track after Zhanna, who was dancing around the curve in celebration.

Confused, she looked over to the stands near the finish line, where some American athletes were sitting, and caught the eye of sprinter Jon Drummond. Thumbs up. She looked at the people around him. More thumbs up. Thumbs up from everybody. She had won in 10.83. Zhanna had been two ticks behind. Five months after returning to the track, Marion was the fastest woman in the world.

Embarrassed when she heard the announcement, Zhanna threw a shoe in the air, then raced back down the track and hugged Marion, who threw her hands in the air, saluted the crowd, ran down the straightaway, and began to cry.

She thought of so many things then, so many people. Of C.J., who had started her thinking she should give track and field another try. Of Trevor and what might have happened if he hadn't come over to her starting blocks that day at Paul Derr Field.

Of Charlie Wells, who had helped pay the bills when she was getting started. Of John Capriotti, who had gone to bat for her at

Nike when others had been skeptical. Of her basketball teammates, who had told her to chase her dreams.

Of her mother and Albert and Ira, who had supported her from the beginning. Of everybody who had known when she was a little girl, just as she had known, that great things were headed her way.

And the people who had thought she was making a mistake? Those who had warned her, discouraged her, tried to hinder her? Was she thinking of them, too, as she stood there on the track with tears running down her face? Of course she was.

THE END OF THE World Championships was almost comical as Marion and Jackie Joyner-Kersee sat by the long-jump pit, laughing at their collective ineptitude.

"I had a much worse performance than Jackie did," Marion said. "At least she made the finals. We were sitting there saying, 'What the heck is going on?' We just laughed at how things weren't clicking that day."

To Trevor, the problem was twofold. First, Marion was on such a high after winning the 100 that she couldn't concentrate. Also, her speed had increased so much during the summer that she no longer had any sense of where she was on the takeoff board. You're going too fast down the runway, he would signal her. Slow down.

Slow down? After running as fast as she could all her life? This long jump is complicated, she thought, and the concept never really struck home. Slow down. Imagine that.

Failing to make the long-jump finals gave Marion the chance to walk back to the practice track and join a U.S. 4×100 relay team that had finished first in the 1996 Olympics. Replacing Gwen Torrence, Marion ran the second leg, taking the baton from Chryste Gaines and handing it off to Inger Miller, who gave it to Gail Devers for the anchor leg. Marion more than held up her end and when she left Athens she had a matched set of gold medals as souvenirs.

A FEW WEEKS AFTER the World Championships, Marion competed in the 100 meters at a meet in Brussels where she set a personal best of 10.76. Well, what do you know? she thought when she saw the time. Trevor was right.

## 5

Late in 1997, after returning home from Europe following the World Championships in Athens, Marion took stock. Her conditioning and her performances on the track her first year back had exceeded her expectations, and, considering how quickly things were coming together, the year ahead held great promise. Her relationship with C.J., whom she was planning to marry in the fall of 1998, couldn't have been better. Charlie Wells had the flood of business deals coming her way under control. Even her dogs were wonderful, she thought with a grin. There was only one more thing to take care of.

"Trevor," she said one day as a practice session was winding up, "why don't we work out in the morning? When I get up, I don't want to think about what I'm going to do. I just want to go to the track."

But he had to work in the morning, said Trevor, who had taken the summer off to go to Europe but now was back at Glaxo Wellcome. "Work here," Marion told him. "Work for me." Trevor gave his employer his notice that day, and soon he had signed a contract with Marion. After four years of running between his job and the track, he was suddenly free to practice his profession full-time.

IN MAY 1998 Marion went to Chengdu, China, in the Szechwan province. It was her second trip to the Far East that season, and she was already off to a blazing start. She had run the 200 in under twenty-two seconds, long jumped more than twenty-three feet, and, at a meet in Osaka three days before arriving in Chengdu, she had run the 100 in 10.79.

The meet was arranged after Chinese sprinter Li Xuemei also ran 10.79, an Asian record, at a meet the previous October in Shanghai. With government backing, Chinese track officials proposed a race to determine the world's fastest woman. They offered handsome appearance fees to a number of top runners and a bonus of more than $120,000 to anyone who could break Florence Griffith Joyner's world record. If Li won, she would receive a bonus of about $12,000. The race lost some of its luster when Gail Devers and Merlene Ottey stayed away, but Marion was game. Sure, it was off the beaten track, but she was already scheduled for three meets in Japan, so why not stop off in China on the way home?

Marion enjoyed the trip, particularly when the mayor of Chengdu threw a big dinner for everyone involved in the meet. She ate course after course from a large revolving tray, a far cry from her stopover in Japan where, unable to eat anything other than rice and bread, she had lost weight.

Marion won the race easily as Li, cracking under the pressure of the huge buildup and the excitement of running before so many fans from her home province, finished fourth. Weeping

with shame during the medal ceremony, Li was surrounded by reporters at the side of the track demanding to know what had gone
wrong.

Marion jumped down from the podium, where she stood with
the second- and third-place finishers, Sevatheda Fynes and Chandra Sturrup, took Li by the arm, pulled her up to the top step, and
raised her arm in the air. The sullen crowd stood and cheered for
Li and her American conqueror. Li hugged Marion, cried some
more, and asked an interpreter to tell her she would always remember her kindness.

The big news out of Chengdu, however, was not Marion's
spontaneous goodwill gesture. It was her time, 10.71, which lowered her personal best by .05 seconds. In the history of the 100-
meter dash, only Florence Griffith Joyner had ever run faster. This
season was going to be something to see.

NINETEEN NINETY-EIGHT was an odd year out in
track and field. The one year in four with neither an Olympics
nor a World Championship, it had no single meet to point for, no
obvious climax to the season bringing all the greatest athletes together in one place. For Marion, it was perfect. Rather than ar-
ranging her schedule to build toward one meet and setting aside
concentrated amounts of time for practice, she could do the one
thing she wanted to do most: compete.

She was getting offers from all over the world, Charlie Wells
told her. Everybody wanted her. What did he want her to do?
Keep me busy, she replied.

When the schedule was finally drawn up, it looked like this: In
February Marion would go to Australia and come home in March
by way of Japan. In April she would compete in North Carolina

and California. In May she would go back to Japan, then to China and Oregon. In June she would go to Finland, Italy, and New Orleans. In July she would go to Austria, Norway, Italy, New York, and Paris. In August she would go to Sweden, Monaco, Switzerland, and Belgium. In September, she would go to Germany, Russia, and South Africa.

In all, she would compete in thirty-seven different events in twenty-seven different meets on five continents. It was an audacious plan, one that was bound to provoke criticism of both Marion and her coach, who had not been a member of the tightly knit and occasionally smug U.S. track and field fraternity long enough to have become fully accepted.

Marion thought she could do it. She was twenty-two years old. She was approaching her physical peak. The big meets during the next three years, and the increasing demands on her time, would force her to scale back. She would never have another chance to travel as much, to compete as often, to learn how to handle the difficult situations that might come up, to prepare herself so thoroughly for the pressure of the World Championships and the Olympics.

And then there was this: If she didn't enter many meets, she couldn't be sure how often she would get a chance to test herself against the best runners in the world, against Merlene Ottey and Gail Devers and anyone else who might burst onto the scene. If there was no single international meet to motivate her, at least there would be the competition.

Trevor thought it was a great idea. Test Marion's speed and jumping ability. Test her endurance. Test her training regimen. Test her support team. And by all means take on all comers.

"People play this game in track and field," he said. "They don't want to compete too much. They don't want to run against this person or that person. But the way Marion was prepared, we wanted her to take on anyone in the world. Not tomorrow. Not later. Today. Now. If you run fast, come on. She's ready. Are you? I really thought she could dominate the world."

He was right. In 1998 Marion ran the 100-meter dash under eleven seconds eighteen times and had the top six times in the world. She ran the third fastest 200 ever and had the top three times in the world. She had the three longest jumps and the best of them, 23-11¾, had not been equaled since 1994. At the end of the year, she was rated number one in the world in all three events, and, for the second straight year, she was named the top female athlete in international track and field.

The year did wonders for Marion's sprint technique—it was becoming automatic now—and for her confidence. During many races, she had the feeling she was pulling away as if the other runners were standing still. And in fact, there were many meets in which there simply was no competition.

Marion saw the paradox. What had been a chief motivating factor for her—the lack of an international championship meet —had acted as a constraint on her competitors. Nearly all the world's best athletes had competed in the 1995 and 1997 World Championships as well as the 1996 Olympics. They were worn out and they were paying the price.

"I could sense a lot of my competitors beginning to get a little frustrated by the fact I was winning by a good amount," Marion said. "At the end of the season, I heard that some of them were saying, 'We're going to get ready for her. We'll have her in '99.' That just motivated me more."

• • •

IT WAS BREATHLESSLY HOT in New Orleans in June when Marion arrived for the U.S. Nationals—just the way she liked it. The higher the temperature, it had always seemed to her, the faster she ran. The more other athletes cramped up and became dehydrated, the more strength she seemed to take from the heat. No one could deny she was on a hot streak in her events, either, and she decided to compete in them all. No sense backing down now.

What struck Marion about the meet was how much it seemed like a homecoming. She had competed in the 1992 Olympic Trials in New Orleans, setting a national high school record in the 200 that still stood and qualifying for the relay berth in Barcelona she had turned down. It's so different now, she thought. From new kid on the block to the one everybody is trying to beat.

The 100 was first and she ran an astonishing series of times: 10.75 in the first heat, 10.71 in the semifinals (tying the personal best she had set in Chengdu), and 10.72 the next day in the finals. "There's a big gap between Marion and the rest of us right now," said Chryste Gaines, who finished second with a personal best of 10.89. "And I don't think she is going to be coming back any time soon."

Even feeling her legs cramp up a bit that night was no big deal—a little massage and she was as good as new. Marion came back to win the 200 and the long jump the same day. For the first time in fifty years, a woman had won three national titles, an achievement that had the crowd on its feet and brought the media running.

For Marion, though, the event lacked the excitement of Indianapolis the year before, and it took her a moment to figure out why. Then it hit her. She had known she would win. She had been so completely and utterly confident that she had felt no tension beforehand and no release afterward. It was, she thought, like a day at the office. If it convinced other people, fine. But she already knew. The way she was performing now, nobody could touch her.

Her subsequent races in Europe reinforced the point: 10.84 in Linz, 10.82 in Oslo, 10.75 in Rome, with a 23-8¾ long jump thrown in for good measure. The Goodwill Games in New York broke the spell a bit. The meet had been billed as a showcase for international track and field in the United States—Merlene Ottey and Zhanna Pintusevich had been lured with appearance bonuses—but when the wind came up, meet officials refused to let them run the other way. Only Marion broke 11 seconds, and her time, 10.90, was one of her slowest of the year.

"We were disappointed," said Marion, who won the 200 in an excellent time, 21.80, the following day. "In Europe, if the wind is blowing they'll turn the race around. The time might be wind-aided, but at least it will be fast."

ON AUGUST 19 Marion suddenly faced the prospect of her first real competition of the year. Christine Arron, who was born in Guadeloupe and was running for France, won the 100 meters at the European championships in Budapest, overtaking European record-holder Irina Privalova of Russia in the final forty meters and finishing in 10.73. Just another runner whose career had been hampered by injuries before the meet began, Arron was suddenly the third fastest woman in history, and her time was only .02 off Marion's personal best. Then, as if to prove she was no fluke, Arron, her hair dyed orange for the occasion, took the French 4×100 relay team from third to first on her anchor leg as she blew past Privalova again in the final fifty meters.

"I now feel in shape to compete on a similar level with Marion Jones," Arron announced after the race.

She didn't have long to wait because in just over a week she and Marion would meet at the 100 meters in Brussels. The race was part of a million-dollar Golden League challenge, sponsored by the International Amateur Athletic Federation, in which every athlete winning a designated event in seven specific meets during the summer would split the huge jackpot. Marion had won all the previous Golden League 100-meter races in 1998 so she would be running not only to beat her new challenger, but also to keep alive her chance for a share of a million dollars.

The European press couldn't get enough of it, particularly since Marion was so clearly in top form. Competing in Europe before Arron's breakthrough performance, she ran 10.88 in Paris, 10.87 in Malmö, 10.72 in Monte Carlo, and 10.77 in Zurich. Then in Lausanne, where she had run poorly and lost to Gail Devers the year before, she ran 10.72, a tick off her personal best and .01 better than Arron's time in Budapest a few days before.

At the pre–meet press conference in Brussels, there was one major line of questioning and at first Marion was properly diplomatic. "I think it's wonderful Christine Arron has run so fast," she said. "I congratulate her and I'm looking forward to running against her."

The reporters were not deterred. Are you concerned about Christine, Marion? She's awfully close to you. Are you worried about Christine? It looks as if she has a chance to beat you. Well, are you *scared* of Christine, then? This journalistic persistence finally had its desired effect.

Trash talk was part of the sprinting game, Marion knew, part of the psychological warfare sprinters waged in the battle for an extra few ticks on the clock. Sprinters are the gunfighters of track and field, and if they can get their opponents to bring a little uncertainty to the duel, so much the better. But Marion had had enough. "Let's just race," she said. She was tired of talking about Christine. "I've heard that some of the articles said I was a little edgy," she said later. "And you know what? After being asked the same question so many times, maybe I was. But when we raced, that said it all."

The race was as matter-of-fact as the buildup had been intense. Running into a headwind, Marion led from the start, opened up a commanding lead, and won in 10.80. Arron finished several strides behind at 10.95, and then it was her turn to be a little edgy. More than a little, in fact.

"She thinks she's unbeatable," *L'Equipe,* the French sports daily, reported Arron as saying several days later. "She's young. Perhaps she has a body of steel, but when she starts to break down it will astonish me if she's so arrogant. The first time she loses, it will really shake her confidence."

The *first* time she loses, Marion wondered. Where did this woman get her information? She had lost plenty of times, and she was certain she would lose again. She had never lost to Christine Arron, though.

Marion was surprised by Arron's level of invective, but she had already begun to feel uncomfortable around some of her competitors. It was more than the typical posturing, she thought. She felt they were blaming her for having dropped out of track and field and then achieving such rapid success on her return. Occasionally she would hear reports that other runners were miffed that she was competing in—and winning—so many events.

Who did she think she was trying to win three events in the U.S. Nationals? It was as if she was trying to take something away from the other athletes.

But the older competitors on the circuit reacted much differently. Jackie Joyner-Kersee, now retired, Gail Devers, Heike Drechsler, and Merlene Ottey had gone out of their way to be welcoming and gracious, even while Marion was beating them. Perhaps this was because they had already won their medals and set their records and felt secure in their accomplishments. "Everybody's always going to love people like Gail and Jackie whether I beat them or not," she said.

Another reason was the veterans' longer view of Marion's accomplishments. Yes, they were losing to her, but in the process she was doing great things for the sport they all loved, and that was to be applauded.

"You can see the excitement when people know Marion is going to compete," said Gail Devers, whose brave battle against Graves' disease, which had nearly caused her legs to be amputated, made her gold medals in the 1992 and 1996 Olympics such a remarkable achievement. "I know when I step into the blocks next to her that nowhere during the race can I back down.

"I think she's one of the people who's going to bring our sport back to the forefront. She's doing what Florence did ten years ago, setting a new standard. I honestly feel what Marion has brought to track and field for women, and what she will bring, is going to be great for years to come."

On September 1, four days after the meet in Brussels, Marion won her sixteenth straight 100-meter dash of the year in Berlin. Christine Arron, who had been entered, withdrew without explanation.

MARION'S MIRACLE SEASON ENDED at the IAAF World Cup meet in Johannesburg, and while she was excited to visit the continent she had dreamed of for so long, she was surprised, too. It was supposed to be hot, she thought, as she noted the seventy-degree temperatures on the track where she would compete in all three of her events.

Marion had been warned about the hazards of running at altitude, but hadn't been particularly impressed. Yeah, yeah, whatever, she replied to those who told her she might not feel well immediately after running. But after competing in her first race, the 200, she understood.

"Are you OK?" C.J. asked her as she came off the track gasping for air.

"Just let me catch my breath," she said as she sat down next to the track. After thirty minutes of being all but unable to move, she was still catching it.

Even her time—21.62, the third fastest 200 ever—didn't completely ease the pain. The fact that it had been achieved at altitude, where the lower air pressure often makes for greater performances, diminished the achievement somewhat in her eyes, as did her annoyance that she had been distracted by one recurring thought. She wanted to go home. The year had been a ball, something she would never forget and never be able to repeat. But enough was enough. It was time to sleep in her own bed, play with her dogs, sit still for a while.

It was even cooler the next day when Marion set another personal best, 10.65, in the 100—the fourth fastest race of all time. She was getting ever closer to Florence Griffith Joyner's ten-year-old sprint records: 10.49 and 21.34. In a year or two, she might be there, she thought, but for now there was just one more event and she could go home at last.

On the final day of the meet, the weather disintegrated altogether: fifty degrees and raining. Great, Marion thought as she prepared for the long jump. Oh, well, it was wet for everybody else, too.

The competition was over almost before it began. Heike Drechsler of Germany, one of the greatest long jumpers in history, got off a strong early jump of 23-2½, and while Marion came within three inches, that was the best she could do. Down to her last jump, she raced down the runway, realized the wind was interfering with her stride, saw her foot hit well over the foul board, and ran through the sand. And that was it. The year to end all years had ended with her only loss, a loss devoid of emotion, excitement, or even a final jump.

The more people tried to tell Marion that the defeat didn't matter, that she'd had a wonderful season and was sure to be named international Athlete of the Year for a second time, the angrier she became. She had done it again, she thought. She had let down mentally in the final meet of the year. In 1997 she lost in the 100 to Merlene Ottey in Tokyo, and she had promised herself it wouldn't happen again.

"At the start of training in '98, I made it a point that I wanted to win my last competition," she said. "I wanted to be able to rise above it when my body and my mind were tired, and I fell short. Again. All I could think about was that long jump and how lousy I competed and how it wasn't me. I can't let that happen to me ever again. Or not very often."

Trevor realized he had learned something, too. He taken things too lightly. He had been lulled by Marion's previous victories into not bothering to have her put in extra work on the long jump. It wasn't the weather, he thought. They had shown up at the meet thinking Marion was going to blow the competition away. And he, too, promised himself it wouldn't happen again.

In the end, though, Marion came to the realization that her season had been defined not by her defeat in the final event but by all the victories that preceded it. "I was satisfied," she said with a smile. "I can even go so far as to say I was happy."

EARLY ONE MORNING, not long after she returned home from Johannesburg, Marion picked up the phone to hear Trevor, in a voice barely above a whisper, tell her that Florence Griffith Joyner was dead at the age of thirty-eight. In shock, she and C.J. sat speechless for ten minutes before turning on the television set for the confirmation neither of them wanted to hear.

"It hurt so much," Marion said. "It hurt because my generation, those of us who are competing now, were so inspired by her. The first time we saw Florence, we were at the stage in our lives where we were very impressionable. To see her compete, to see her break records, and to see her enjoy it so much—to be so confident, so strong—it hurt. I never met her, but I knew her. We all knew her."

Several months later, Marion went to New York to receive her second Jesse Owens Award as the outstanding woman track athlete in the United States. Also accepting an award in his wife's honor was Al Joyner, the former Olympic triple jump champion.

"Like the skin was being ripped off my body," he said of the sensation he felt when he rose to speak. "But at the same time, I don't want the pain to go away because that would mean she wasn't with me anymore."

Al was Florence's coach when she broke the world record in the 100 and 200 in 1988, and he had seen it coming in practice.

"I told Florence she was going to run 10.5," he said, "because that's what I was running and she was beating me."

"If I run that fast, they'll dissect me," Florence joked. She did and they did.

No number of drug tests—not even one the same day at the 1988 Olympics in Seoul when Ben Johnson was caught using steroids—could quell the rumors that Florence must have been using performance-enhancing drugs. Neither could an autopsy. The proven incidence of drug use in track and field, and the rumors about those who aren't caught, had left people profoundly cynical. How many reporters who cover the sport believe Florence was using illegal drugs? a prominent sportswriter was asked not long after she died. All of them, he replied.

"It never bothered Florence," Al Joyner said. "It bothered me. All the people who attacked her, she never said a word against them. All she said was she was going to pray for them. But what do they want? For God to come down and say she was clean? Even that wouldn't be enough for some people. Why can't they let her rest in peace?"

From the beginning, Florence and Al were tickled by Marion. Tickled that she walked off the track with such a promising career ahead of her and played basketball simply because she wanted to. Tickled that she came back from her serious injuries the way Al's sister Jackie had fought her way back. If anything, they thought, Marion might be tougher mentally than Jackie was at her age, and that was saying a lot.

But the moment they truly came to admire Marion was when she stood up and said she meant to break Florence's records.

"I was waiting for the first time somebody asked her about it," Al said. "I wanted to see how she handled it. She was the first one not to be intimidated. And the way she answered the question, with such style. She said, 'As I get older and better, the

records will fall. I'm still learning.' She seemed so quiet and confident. Florence said that because she said she could break it, she'd
probably be the one."

Not long after Florence died, Al realized his thinking had
changed. Now he not only thought Marion would break the
records, he hoped she would. People had said Florence had set the
records because she used drugs, he thought. They said no one
could run that fast. But now the same people were saying Marion might break the records. "Which is it?" Al said. "One person
could run this fast, but another person couldn't? I think Marion
will certify the records."

Marion knows that if she does break Florence's records, she
will come under suspicion, too.

"I've heard women on the circuit say they don't think it's possible for a woman to run faster than 10.6 clean," Marion said.
"These are women running my event saying that. So I know if I
break world records that there are going to be people who say I'm
on drugs. And I accept that. I guess it's part of running fast."

The entire business of drug testing is such a muddle, she said,
such a mixture of rumors and confusion and strict procedures
that never quite seem to be followed. Though out-of-season testing is supposed to be random, she and C.J. found officials parked
at their door at least ten times when they returned from practice
in the months after the 1998 season had ended. Several times
Marion was tested twice in the same week. Random? Hardly.

And the potential for misunderstanding, for some dreadful
mistake, always seems to be present, particularly on the international circuit where the officials speak languages she doesn't understand, and write down who knows what on their clipboards. It
makes her feel uneasy.

"And there are times when they do the most embarrassing things," she said. "Like having somebody standing right in front of you making you take off all your clothes—underwear, socks, everything—and you have to stand there stark naked and go to the bathroom in front of them."

As for banned substances, the list is not only endless, it is constantly changing. Any new doctor's prescription, or even over-the-counter medicine, must first be cleared with a drug hotline to see if it's banned. Sometimes the fear of illegal substances can be almost comical. Some athletes avoid food supplements on the theory that it's hard to know what's in them. Others won't drink herbal teas because of a rumor that somebody once failed a test because of them. Rumors reign.

"I've heard that sesame seeds might create something you can come up positive for," Marion said. "Really, I mean it. It's just a rumor, but I stay away. No sesame seed bagels. Or poppy seed either. I'm not taking any chances."

After a time, Marion said, athletes learn not to ask questions because the suspicion can be turned back on them. "They seem to be saying, 'If you're clean, why are you questioning it?'" she said. "So we learn to keep our mouths shut. All I can do is continue to be clean and to be around people who are clean. It's sad, though, isn't it? Everybody wants you to run fast, but once you do there's suspicion. It's kind of a dead-end road either way."

AT THE JESSE OWENS Award dinner, Marion had something else to say about Florence Griffith Joyner and it made Al Joyner cry.

"Al," she said, "Florence won't be forgotten. She's going to live through me."

## Part 2

## *The Season*

# 6

The new season began where the old one had ended, in Africa. The meet was in Roodeport, a Johannesburg suburb not far from the track where Marion's perfect 1998 season had come undone, and she was anxious to get started. First, though, there was something else she was looking forward to: another youth clinic in Soweto.

Prior to the World Cup the previous September, Marion had participated in an IAAF-sponsored opening of a community center in the black township, and, as it was winding down, it had all turned into such a wonderful goof.

Marion had asked a Nike official for one hundred T-shirts to pass out, but when she arrived she saw the kids were already wearing T-shirts from Adidas, Nike's biggest rival, which had been provided by the IAAF. No need to cause a fuss, Marion thought. The Nike T-shirts stayed in the car. When it was time to leave, though, she discovered dozens of kids outside the community center who had been turned away because of lack of space.

"Drive real slow," she told the driver of their small van, and soon they were ripping open the boxes of T-shirts and flinging them out the windows to the ecstatic children who ran after them as they drove down the road. "I think some of the IAAF and Adidas people might have been a little upset," Marion said, "but it wasn't about that. Those kids were having a ball."

Now, IT WAS SIX months later, and the Soweto clinic was more elaborate. Instead of an indoor venue, the site was a large stadium and the guest list contained a number of other athletes, including Olympic champion Michael Johnson and Marion's teammates Antonio Pettigrew and Jerome Young.

Marion was disappointed once again to see youngsters on the outside looking in. Only a handful had been chosen to participate in the clinic, and hundreds of others sat in the stands behind a fence with a guard stationed at the gate. While Marion and the other athletes demonstrated techniques on the field, C.J. and Trevor went into the stands and chatted with some of those who had been left out.

As the day ended, the kids who had been in the clinic lined up for autographs. Marion looked up and saw that those who had been excluded would continue to be kept at a distance. No clinic, no autographs, nothing. This is so unfair, she thought. She wasn't going anywhere. She had plenty of time to sign autographs and talk. Then she looked up again and saw that C.J. had read her mind.

Placing his 320-pound frame squarely in front of the guard, C.J. swung the gate open, smiled broadly, and waved the kids through. Within minutes, the field was flooded with youngsters who had been pent up in the stands for more than an hour and were now bearing down on the athletes signing autographs on the field.

There was a fair amount of pushing and shoving, and a lot of noise, but clinic officials helped hold the crowd back and tried to form it into orderly lines as the athletes signed autographs. Marion handed out cards with her picture on them, and many of the youngsters—none more than four feet tall, it seemed—pushed them back across the table for her to sign.

And then she saw the man with the belt.

A teacher at a Soweto school, he had reacted to the students' exuberance by taking off his belt and swinging it at the hands of those who were extending Marion's cards across the table too aggressively to suit him.

"Get back! Get back!" he shouted as the children he hit yelped in pain while others cringed.

"Stop it!" Marion shouted at the man, who was only a few feet away.

Unheeding, he drew the belt back to lash at another child. Marion rose from her chair, reached out, pulled the belt from his hands, stared at it for a moment, then flung it across the field. At that instant, it was hard to tell who seemed most upset—the teacher whose authority had been challenged, or the young woman who had seen such ugliness.

"Don't you ever do that!" she shouted. "You should never do that! They just wanted autographs. They weren't hurting anybody!"

Shaken, Marion left the stadium with the cheers of the children ringing in her ears. Three days later in Roodeport, she easily won a 200-meter race. Her 1999 season, the most important of her life to date, was under way.

THE RUNNING TRACK of Paul Derr Field on the North Carolina State campus is occupied by kids playing, elderly joggers, and middle-aged women chatting during their power strolls. Marion goes all but unnoticed. She is asked for her autograph no more than once a day. The morning exercisers wander through adjacent lanes without recognizing her. Her workout proceeds with no interruption from the world outside, or from the basketball-mad world she inhabits.

Once, a reporter and camera crew from CBS television came to Raleigh, and, as they rode from the airport to the track, their cabdriver asked whom they were going to interview.

"Marion Jones, the world track champion," was the reply.

"I don't know about track champion," the driver said, "but I know she was the point guard for the '94 team that won the NCAA basketball championship."

As odd as this setting may seem—one can only imagine the mob scene that would greet, say, Venus and Serena Williams practicing at a public tennis court—it is perfect for Marion and the other athletes who work with Trevor. Paul Derr Field is a short ride from Marion's house and the facilities are superb: an all-weather quarter-mile track, an excellent long-jump runway and pit, and a comfortable shed in which to store gear and, when necessary, get in out of the rain.

During most of the practice sessions, Trevor is something of a ringmaster, orchestrating one set of workouts for his middle-distance runners, another for his hurdlers, and another for Marion, who often works in tandem with Chandra Sturrup. On summer days, Trevor's young son and daughter may tag along, placing one more demand on his attention. Add the occasional visitor—a Nike representative with shoes for Marion to try, a reporter who has arranged an interview after her workout, one or two people simply enjoying the sun—and it can all seem slightly chaotic.

But not to Marion, who, once her workout begins, isolates herself from the surrounding elements. Whether working on an aspect of the sprints or her long-jump approach, there is a sense of total, almost grim, determination that seems to remove her from whatever is going on around her. Marion's teammates have long since come to recognize the unseeing stare of concentration on her face at moments like these and have learned not to bother her as long as it remains. Then, as if a switch has been flipped in her mind, she is back among them, smiling, talking, kidding around. Sometimes with a vengeance.

Sitting in the shed behind the track one rainy afternoon, Marion relates a story she has heard about a man who was trapped alone in the forest under a fallen tree and cut off his leg with a penknife to get free.

"Would you cut your leg off?" she asks.

"No way," Trevor says and the others agree. "I'm gone."

"If it was your leg or your *life*?" Marion insists, and then she ups the ante by asking her teammates if they would resort to cannibalism if necessary, an idea she got from the movie *Alive*. Trevor and the others react in horror, but Marion persists.

"You mean if Antonio was right there," she says, pointing to Antonio Pettigrew who is lying on his back as Trevor massages a leg cramp, "and a big piece of his butt was there, you wouldn't eat it? Just like a piece of beef jerky? Just a piece off the top? If it meant staying alive?"

"Whoa!" Trevor shouts. "I'm not going to Europe with Marion. If the plane goes down, she's going to eat us."

• • •

IN CONTRAST TO HER globe-trotting in 1998, Marion began her 1999 season slowly. There were only three meets on her schedule before June and she cut back on the number of events in which she would compete during the summer. Much of the schedule was built around two considerations.

The first was the fact that the 200 meters was a 1999 Golden League event so another share of a million-dollar jackpot would be hers if she could win at that distance in seven designated meets. Marion's victories in the 100 in 1998 had given her a third of the prize and, when the first-place money from each individual race was added in, her total Golden League take had been about $750,000. Marion was unbeaten in the 200 since returning to the track in 1997, so another large bonus payoff was very much within reach.

The second consideration was even more important: the biennial World Track and Field Championships to be held in August in Seville, Spain. Coming almost exactly a year before the 2000 Olympics, they would be the first test of her bold, some would say foolhardy, quest to win five gold medals in Sydney.

JESSE OWENS AND Carl Lewis, the greatest track and field athletes of their day, are the only men in their sport to have won four gold medals in a single Olympics. Fanny Blankers-Koen of Holland is the only woman. But Marion's decision to try to win four gold medals in Seville and five at the Olympics was based not on what others had done in the past, but on what she was doing at the moment.

It all seemed so simple. In 1997 she won two titles at the U.S. Track and Field Championships in Indianapolis and two more at the World Championships in Athens. In 1998 she won three U.S.

titles in New Orleans and was number one in the world in three events: the 100 and 200 meters, and the long jump. So why not add a relay to her repertoire for the 1999 World Championships in Seville, and then one more for the Olympics a year later?

"It's just a natural progression," Marion said as she sat in a chair by the side of the track. "It didn't cross my mind that nobody had ever done it. My feeling was I'm sitting on top of the world athletically. I'm fit, I'm healthy, I'm happy. So five golds looked very, very possible."

When Marion did realize the historic implications of her plan, her incentive grew. "I want to do something that nobody's ever done," she said. "I want to be remembered when I'm long gone."

The possibility of setting world records played a part in this as well. "All the greats," she said, "Carl Lewis, Evelyn Ashford, Florence Griffith Joyner, Jackie Joyner-Kersee, Jesse Owens, they're who they are not only because of their consistency, but also because they were better than anybody before them. So that's more of wanting to do something that's never been done. People ask when the records are going to fall. I say I'll be around until they do."

As Marion assessed her chances for Seville, it was easy to see that, barring injury, she would be a heavy favorite at both 100 and 200 meters. She was the second fastest woman in history in both events, and, among her current competitors, no one was close.

The long jump was more of a problem. Her leap of 23-11¾ in a meet at Eugene, Oregon, in 1998 was the best in the world during the past four years, and there were those who thought she might one day do what Bob Beamon had done for the men's event in the 1968 Olympics: set a world record that would last for a generation.

But, despite her success in 1998, the long jump was still her most inconsistent event. She hadn't begun competing until her senior year in high school and, because of basketball, hadn't been able to give it the attention it deserved at North Carolina. So although her speed and power had made her the top long jumper in the world, she was still essentially a novice with much to learn. That was one of the things she liked about it.

"It's a challenge," Marion said. "People are saying, 'Yeah, she can run, but her jumping needs work.'" These comments only made her want to continue practicing, to continue learning a little more every day. One day, she believes, it will all come together. And then, watch out.

Marion's decision to run the $4 \times 400$ relay at the World Championships in Seville was strategic. As the fastest woman in the world, she would be an automatic choice for the $4 \times 100$ relay in the 2000 Olympics, but a fifth gold medal would depend on the longer race. "I've never run the four by four in a major competition," she said, "so we thought it would be best for me, and for the team, if I could get a little experience before getting thrown in with the alligators in 2000."

Though some track experts think she could be number one in the world in the 400 if she trained for it, Marion seldom runs the distance, and for one very good reason. She hates it.

"It just hurts too much," she said. "I have no control of my body afterwards. I can't breathe, I can't sit, I can't walk. I like running the relay. It's a completely different feeling when you're trying to chase somebody down. But I've never learned how to run the open four hundred meters, and I don't care if I never do."

Marion's participation in the 400 had already turned her one race at that distance in 1999 into something of a farce. In April she went to the Mount San Antonio College Relays outside Los Angeles. Her brother, Albert, drove in from Oxnard, and a number of her high school teammates, coaches, and friends also showed up for her one California appearance of the year. But in the hours before the race, seven runners dropped out.

"The day before, I had a full race," Scott Davis, the meet director, said. "Then, a couple of coaches came up and said their athletes weren't ready. Weren't ready to face Marion was my interpretation. I was really scrambling there at the end. We had only five people on the track."

Most disappointing to Marion was the fact that Falilat Ogunkoya of Nigeria, who had posted the top 400 time in the world in 1998, chose to run the 200, although Davis, trying to be fair, said Ogunkoya hadn't formally committed to either event. "It seems to me you'd want to run against the best," he said. "If you get your ass kicked, you get your ass kicked. So what?"

Virtually unopposed, Marion ran the distance in 50.79, the second fastest time of the year in the world to that point, and more than good enough to earn a spot on the 4×400 relay team in Seville.

TAKING A BREAK from practice, Marion watches a middle-aged man practicing his form over a lone hurdle on the track. Struck by a thought, she turns to Trevor.

"Trev," she says, "if I set up the hurdles now, how fast could I go?"

Trevor turns and waves across the track to C.J.

"Six!" he shouts. "She's going for six!"

"What?" C.J. yells back.

"Six gold medals!"

"Don't start that rumor," Marion says, laughing. "Don't go there."

SITTING BY THE SIDE of the track cooling down from her workout, Marion speaks quietly of the season ahead, and of Seville, which will be the true starting point toward the Sydney Olympics.

"New Orleans was wonderful," she says of her three gold medals in the 1998 U.S. Nationals, "but I look back on it and think I could have done more. I don't know how it feels yet to be there, to have arrived. When I win the four in Seville, I want them to be good performances. And when I win the five in Sydney, I want them to be great performances. Once I do that, I'll start smelling the flowers at the top. Just a couple of them, though."

MARION'S FIRST EUROPEAN meet of the summer was on June 10 in Helsinki and it also marked her first trip on the Concorde. The cost was outrageous, but the benefits were considerable. Since her body would not have to adjust to crossing numerous time zones, a process that can take days, she could fly in, compete a day later, then come home and continue training without a break.

Marion was excited about flying in the supersonic aircraft, and, like many first-time Concorde flyers, she was surprised the plane was so small.

"You should have seen her stealing those big folders they give you," C.J. teased her.

"I did not!" she replied in mock exasperation. "I took some pens—my pen, C.J.'s pen, and the seat next to me didn't have anybody in it so I took that pen. We have a problem losing pens."

"She lost two of them, too," C.J. said. "We still only have one pen."

Marion easily won the 200 in Helsinki in an excellent time, 21.91. She had already run the distance in 21.81 at the Prefontaine Classic in Eugene, Oregon, ten days earlier, so her chances of earning the Golden League bonus in Europe later in the summer looked strong.

Under normal circumstances, the Helsinki meet would have been her last competition before the U.S. Track and Field Championships in Eugene two weeks later. But on June 12, the day after flying home, she entered the long jump in the Pontiac Grand Prix Invitational, a meet that attracted only a few elite American athletes and offered relatively modest appearance fees and prize money.

One of the attractions for Marion was that it was held in conjunction with the two-day national high school track and field championships, an event that brought together thousands of young athletes from around the country. Marion retains warm memories of her high school track days, and a few months earlier she had contributed a large sum to cover travel expenses for young athletes to compete in the Nike Indoor Classic in Columbus, Ohio.

A second reason she wanted to compete in the meet was that it took place at home. Marion could park her gear in the shed at Paul Derr Field, and her car next door, warm up on the track where she practices daily, and jump from the runway she knows best. With friends, family, and fans helping to fill the 3,000-seat bleachers, she could also give a boost to track and field where she lives.

It was a beautiful afternoon, the crowd was large and enthusiastic, and the high school athletes added energy and excitement to the day. The track was intimate, as usual. Pine trees ring the area, and passengers in cars on the road above could look down and wave. Delighted to be able to get in some badly needed long-jump competition, Marion wasn't at all bothered by the fact that the field wasn't particularly strong.

After one jump, she was losing.

Adrien Sawyer of Texas A&M, the eleventh best long jumper in the United States in 1998, jumped 22-4½ to take the lead. This was quickly noted by the public-address announcer describing the action from the other side of the track and urging the crowd to cheer for the hometown favorite. The announcements became more insistent on Marion's subsequent attempts, but they didn't help; her second jump left her three inches short of Sawyer, and the next two were foul.

As Marion stood at the head of the runway for her fifth jump, the announcer fairly begged the crowd to support her in her hour of need—"She needs your help!"—and she responded with her best jump of the day. It, too, was just barely foul.

Waiting to take her sixth and final jump, Marion had two thoughts. Losing to Heike Drechsler, an Olympic champion, in Johannesburg after a grueling year of competition was one thing, but losing to an unheralded athlete on her home track would be a huge embarrassment. All right, so it's not the biggest meet in the world, she told herself. But losing is losing, whether it's in the World Championships or in Raleigh. When it's time to jump, it's time to jump.

Her second thought was more encouraging. Two of her three fouls had been excellent jumps—possibly even personal bests—and she hadn't been very far over the foul line. She still had a good jump, a really good jump, in her, she told herself, and the excitement started to build.

"I'm having a little trouble getting my steps right," she told Trevor as she approached the head of the runway.

"Look," he said, "forget everything we've been working on, all right? Let's move your start half a foot back, and then blast it! Give it all you've got. When you're in the air, then you can worry about technique."

From the moment she took off and the official's white flag signaled a fair jump, there was no doubt Marion had won. At twenty-three feet even, she was far beyond Sawyer, and only half an inch off the best long jump in the world to that point in the year, by Fiona May of Italy. The announcer all but screamed the happy news and the crowd erupted in cheers for the thrilling last-jump victory.

Marion lay huddled in the pit, clutching her right knee. The pain was bad, but the fear was worse.

Marion knew something was wrong before she landed. She was coming down with her legs under her, almost as if she were standing, rather than in the standard half-sitting position with her legs in front. It is a natural flaw in her style, one that has troubled her since she first long jumped in high school, and one she has worked hard to eliminate. In the excitement of her final effort, she forgot about technique and didn't rotate her body enough to get her legs out front. She was particularly annoyed at herself because her five previous landings had been so much better.

Making matters worse, Marion came down in an area of the pit that hadn't been raked, perhaps because nobody had jumped that far all afternoon. The sand was packed hard and didn't give way when she landed, which would have allowed her leg to slide forward. Her knee locked, twisting back and to the side.

Marion had had nightmares like this: She is standing up and

somebody in front of her is kicking her knee, kicking it backward until it breaks. But now it was not a nightmare. Now it was happening and as her knee began to swell, her fear began to mount.

First, though, she had to get out of the pit without spoiling her mark in the sand. They haven't registered the jump yet, she told herself. She hadn't officially won. She started to move forward when C.J., who had been sitting alongside the runway and had hurried over, picked her up and began to carry her out of the pit.

"Put me down," she said, eyes flashing, and he quickly obeyed.

Let's just see how bad it is, she thought. Let's all just take a deep breath and determine the extent of the damage. The last thing we need is a stadium full of people watching C.J. carry me out of the long-jump pit. "I can just see it on the Internet now," she said later. "'Marion Jones can't walk.' I wanted to dispel that rumor before it started."

C.J. and Chris Whetstine, her massage therapist, produced a large bag of ice from a cooler and soon Marion was sitting on the grass behind the long-jump runway with her knee encased in ice. Chris massaged her toes and fended off several doctors who came down from the stands to offer their services.

"Poor Chris," Marion said. "Everybody wants to touch. But I didn't want anybody else because they could easily go around giving a false diagnosis, and that's the worst thing that could happen. I have total faith in Chris. If he said, 'Marion, I think you need a physician's opinion, OK.'"

But Chris quickly assured himself there were no fractures or soft-tissue damage, and soon Marion was feeling less pain, even when he pushed her right leg completely over her head while she was lying on her back.

For an hour, Marion sat on the grass with her leg wrapped in ice and told reporters that the injury was nothing serious—a simple hyperextension of the knee. She was excited about her victory, she said, and proud of the Raleigh-Durham community for supporting the meet so extravagantly. All the while, she was surrounded by high school athletes who took turns kneeling down in groups to ask for autographs and have their pictures taken with her.

If she was worried about the extent of her injury, or how it might affect her performance in the upcoming U.S. Nationals in Eugene, she wasn't showing it. Rather, she was smiling and chatting with anyone who came by. Her responsibility now was to the media and the kids. In the meantime, the bag of ice stayed snugly in place.

WHAT MARION NEEDED NOW was a variety of treatments for her injured knee: ice, massage, acupuncture, chiropractic manipulation, tight wraps to keep the swelling down, and an MRI exam to determine the extent of the damage. What she did not need, although she prescribed it for herself anyway, was a trip to Syracuse to visit her former North Carolina basketball teammate, Melissa Johnson.

Melissa had grown depressed her sophomore year after feeling misled by the coaching staff about her role on the basketball team. As she tried to decide what to do (she ultimately transferred to Harvard), Marion counseled and consoled her, drawing on her own difficult decision to leave the Tar Heels. Melissa's father, who was particularly grateful for Marion's concern, called several times to thank her, and soon the whole Johnson family had joined Marion's circle of friends. In the fall of 1998 Melissa and her parents attended Marion's wedding to C.J.

The day before Marion flew to Helsinki, and while Melissa was unreachable at a Harvard-affiliated wilderness leadership trip in the White Mountains of New Hampshire, Melissa's father died. Disturbed that she hadn't been able to attend the funeral, worried about her friend, and realizing her summer competition schedule was inflexible, Marion saw the few days after the Raleigh meet as her only chance to visit.

"Marion, you're so busy," Melissa said when Marion called from Helsinki. "You have a meet this weekend, don't you?"

"After the meet," Marion insisted. "Is it okay if I come?"

"Are you asking my permission? Of course, it's okay. I'd love to see you. You'll stay with us."

"No, no, I'll just stay in a hotel. Don't even tell your mom I'm coming. I know what she must be going through, relatives and stuff. I just want to hang out with you for a couple days."

"Marion, that's ridiculous. The relatives will be gone. You'll stay with us."

"Well, I don't want you to feel like you have to entertain me or anything."

"Enter*tain* you? Does that mean I should cancel the circus?"

Once the media retreated to the press box and the high school athletes finally had their fill of pictures and autographs, Marion lay down on Chris's massage table for a few moments, then changed clothes in the shed and prepared to leave for the airport.

C.J. asked Marion to reconsider the trip, and Chris was concerned that a long plane ride, during which her knee would have to remain relatively immobile, would aggravate the inflammation. At least she's flying first class, he thought, and will be able to stretch her leg.

Only Trevor, unflappable as ever, seem unconcerned. "She's a big girl," he said. "She'll call if there's a problem."

As for Marion, it was not an issue. She had told Melissa she was coming and she was coming. It was as simple as that. So only a few hours after injuring her knee, Marion drove to the Raleigh-Durham airport, flew to Washington, changed planes, and continued on to Syracuse. As Chris had predicted, her knee began to swell during the trip and Marion realized she hadn't bothered to have it wrapped, which would have helped control the inflammation. A big mistake, she realized.

Marion negotiated the unfamiliar streets of Syracuse in a rental car late at night, while Melissa, who had spoken several times during the evening with a worried C.J., wished she hadn't let Marion talk her out of picking her up at the airport. When Marion finally arrived, it was shortly before midnight. Melissa met her at the door with a bag of ice and a hug.

THE NEXT MORNING Melissa wasn't so sure about the visit. Marion shouldn't be here, she told her mother. She should be in North Carolina seeing a doctor.

After prying some of the details of the injury out of Marion, after seeing how uncomfortable she was with her knee constantly elevated and wrapped in ice, and after several phone conversations with C.J., Melissa's strongest feeling was one of guilt. Nor did sitting with Marion and watching the taped broadcast of the Raleigh meet the previous day help. The way Marion's knee bent as she landed seemed grotesque, Melissa thought, almost hideous. "It made me want to throw up," she said. "And she was just sitting there giving interviews like nothing was wrong."

"Marion, should we take you in to see somebody?" Barbara Johnson, a retired operating-room head nurse, asked. "It's Sunday, but I can find somebody. Or there's the emergency room."

"No," Marion said. "I'm fine. I don't want to see anyone. I came here to see you guys."

And for the next two days, that's what she did. Marion and Melissa went to the mall—where one of their purchases was a knee wrap—to the movies and to lunch. They swam in the Johnsons' pool and went to a gym where they renewed a weight-lifting partnership that had begun in Chapel Hill. Six feet five and very lean, Melissa had needed to gain weight, and the North Carolina strength coach had teamed her up with Marion, one of the team's most dedicated lifters.

This is like old times, Melissa told herself, and for the first time she began to feel less guilty about the visit. Marion was relaxed, joking about this and that, and she realized what Marion had known instinctively all along. Yes, she had come to see her friend, but she had also come for herself. What her knee needed for the next few days—ice, elevation, tight wraps—was as available in Syracuse as in Raleigh. What she needed was a few days off.

"It's nice to be here and not have to do anything," Marion said. "It's nice not to have to be somewhere at this o'clock and that o'clock."

"Marion is so far from a drama queen," Melissa said. "Some of the stuff we did was so low key. I showed her my high school. We saw my best buddy who works in a grocery store. We ran into a bunch of kids walking out of the movies that I knew from high school, and she didn't want to be introduced as Marion Jones. She wanted to be 'This is my friend Marion' and leave it at that."

Two days later, Marion flew home to a battery of tests, a grueling rehabilitation regimen, an anxious husband, and a coach who had ten days to prepare her for the biggest American track meet of the year.

*(Clockwise from top right) Marion and C.J.; On the way to the wedding in Raleigh with her brother Albert; Practicing starts during spring training; Blasting out of the blocks.*

*(Clockwise from top right)
Marion taking the baton from
Inger Miller at the Penn Relays;
Marion celebrates a 1999 Penn
Relays win in the 4×200-meter
relay; Marion with track fan
Bill Cosby; In 1999, President
Nelson Mandela invited
Marion and sprinters Michael
Johnson and Frankie Fredericks
to a reception at his home.*

*(Clockwise from top right) Winning the 200 meters at the 1999 U.S.A. Track and Field Championships; Marion collapses to the track during the 200 meters at the 1999 World Championships in Seville; Another foul in the long jump at the nationals; Marion injures her knee at the Pontiac Grand Prix Invitational.*

(Top) Marion moments after crossing the finish line in the 100 meters at Seville, a world champion again; (Bottom) Marion at the medal ceremony.

## 7

Hayward Field, an aging structure on the University of Oregon campus in Eugene, seemed more like the site of a county fair than of a major national sports championship.

Hot dogs, popcorn, and red licorice vines were sold at weathered wooden kiosks by senior citizens wearing Oregon Ducks caps. Girls in their early teens wandered through the bleachers in pairs selling programs. Spectators parked on residential streets a block or two from the stadium, paid as little as ten dollars for admission, entered through the same gate as the athletes, and never came close to filling the seven thousand seats during the four days of USA Track & Field Outdoor Championships.

A major topic of conversation as the meet began was a calendar of photographs—artistically composed and elegantly reproduced—that showed a dozen of America's top women athletes in the nude. A predictable debate ensued over whether the women were allowing themselves to be exploited, or were celebrating their self-confidence and physical prowess instead. The objections weren't particularly heated, though, and perhaps the final judgment on the calendar, whose proceeds went to charity, was passed by the mother of one of its subjects, Amy Acuff, a long-limbed high-jump champion. "I close down during the high-jump competition," said Mrs. Acuff, who was in charge of a small sales force that sold the calendar from a booth near the track.

Marion had not been asked to appear in the calendar and would have declined in any case. "Not my thing," she said, indicating she thought some pictures were best left untaken.

A more pressing concern for Marion was the weather. Cold and wet, it created running and jumping surfaces that promised slips and falls. Hardly what an athlete still recovering from a knee injury would choose while trying to defend two national titles and qualify for the World Championships.

The fact that Marion's first event was the long jump did not work in her favor, either. She had hurt her knee while jumping in the first place, and the greatest potential for reinjury would be through another jolt in the landing pit. It would have been better for her to run the 200 first, a race she hadn't lost anywhere in the world since her return to the track two years earlier and one with less risk of further trauma.

One piece of luck that did go Marion's way was the fact that she didn't have to run the 100; her victory in the previous World Championships, in Athens in 1997, had automatically qualified her for Seville. Some fans complained that they wanted to see her defend all three of her national titles, but the free pass was a blessing. This was not 1997 in Indianapolis, which had marked Marion's triumphant return to track, or 1998 in New Orleans, where she had turned in the performance of the half-century. This was a matter of survival, of not aggravating her injury, of staying on the road to Seville.

Marion's physical status as she prepared to compete in the long jump on the second day of the meet was still troubling. The MRI exam she had undergone after returning home from Syracuse contained good news: no ligament damage, only a small amount of fluid, a minor bone bruise that would quickly heal. She and C.J. had sighed in relief when they heard the results.

But her knee was still sore. Steve Bernabeu, her chiropractor from Fairfax, Virginia, who had flown down to help with the re- covery, was concerned about her inability to bend her knee back as far as she normally could. Flexibility is one of Marion's prime attributes and while acupuncture and manipulation helped, it was clear she would not be at full strength for the meet.

None of this mattered to Marion. Yes, her knee was sore. No, she would not be 100 percent. But she was anxious to get going. Missing a week of training before such an important meet had been aggravating, particularly when C.J., who was also competing for a spot in the World Championships, would go off to his work- outs and leave her home to wrap her knee and pack it in ice. "It killed me," Marion said of the inactivity. "I felt like I was losing my mind."

And besides, how many times had she played basketball on a sprained ankle? How many times had she had to take it easy in practice, but been ready to go when the whistle blew? When it's time to compete, it's time to compete.

In part, Marion's competitive instincts were at work. But she was also buoyed by a recent phone conversation with someone who knew exactly what she was going through.

"That landing didn't look so good," Jackie Joyner-Kersee told her of the final jump in Raleigh.

"No kidding," Marion laughed.

She once had a similar injury, said Jackie, who had recently re- tired. She hyperextended her knee while running the hurdles, and the pain and swelling were so bad she cried out of fear that her career might be over. But an MRI showed no lasting damage, and doctors told her she could continue training through the injury. And soon enough, she was as good as new.

Marion was touched by Jackie's call, which lifted her spirits and convinced her she would be fine once the meet started. She'd had enough of worrying, enough of coddling herself. She was sick of people asking how's the knee, how's the knee? She didn't care what anybody thought. She was *glad* the long jump was first on the program. She wanted to get it out of the way. She wanted to win, to move on to the 200 and be done with it. She wanted to prove to everybody, and to herself, that she was OK. Let's start worrying about my performances, she told herself, not about my injury.

THE DAY BEFORE the meet began, Marion and her teammates set up shop under a large awning just inside the main gate, which provided easy access to a practice track behind them. This made it possible for anyone entering the grounds to walk right up to where they loosened up, received massages before their events, or just sat and chatted.

It was a scene unimaginable in any other sport, the equivalent of baseball fans being invited into the dugout to mingle with players limbering up before the World Series. But Marion's privacy—and that of Michael Johnson, Maurice Greene, Gail Devers, and the rest of America's greatest track and field stars— was seldom disturbed by spectators wanting to talk, ask for autographs, or simply gawk.

It is hard to explain exactly why track and field is at such a low ebb in the United States; why, as Marion was making her 37-event tour of the world in 1998, she competed only five times in her own country. Unlike soccer, a sport in which Americans have never competed at a high level, most of history's greatest track athletes have been Americans. From Jim Thorpe to Jesse Owens to Edwin Moses to Carl Lewis—and from Babe Didrickson to Wilma Rudolph to Evelyn Ashford to Jackie Joyner-Kersee—Americans have won Olympic gold medals, set world records, and dominated the sport.

But the last time a major international track meet other than the Olympics was held in the United States was more than thirty years ago. The best international track stars almost never compete in this country. With the exception of a few scattered meets here and there, neither do the top Americans.

Lewis Johnson, a former runner who is now a track commentator for NBC, tells of the time he flew off to a meet in Italy with twenty-five dollars in his pocket. When his ground transportation went awry, he was down to his last few lire and frustrated by the knowledge that waiting for him at his hotel were free room and board, a substantial amount of appearance money, and the chance to win more. At home, meanwhile, he was slowly going broke.

The man charged with trying to improve this situation is Craig Masback, a former sub-four-minute miler who went to Princeton, Yale Law School, and Oxford, and who became CEO of USA Track & Field in 1997. He does not underestimate the enormity of his task.

Track and field, Masback likes to say, was the most major of America's minor sports in the 1960s, a time when the sports marketing industry was in its infancy and beginning to be exploited by virtually every other sport. For U.S. track officials, however, it was business as usual, and the result is that except during the Olympics track has all but disappeared from the American consciousness.

One of Masback's goals is to increase corporate sponsorship;

another is to set up a cluster of indoor and outdoor meets early in the year with sufficient appearance and prize money to lure the top American athletes. Though he has been moderately successful in realizing the former objective—General Motors, Adidas, and other companies have become sponsors—the latter may never occur on the scale Masback would like.

The major European meets are long-standing events that draw tens of thousands of fans; they are as much circuses as athletic contests. Cowbells announce the next race, whistles blow as the sprinters race down the track, light shows keep the customers entertained, fans spontaneously cheer "Ser-gei *Bub*-ka! Ser-gei *Bub*-ka!" as the great Russian pole vaulter charges down the runway. It is a revelation to U.S. athletes when they are treated like conquering heroes themselves, and when the best of them are paid extremely well.

"I get off the plane and kids are running up to me," Marion said. "We've gone places where I threw my shoes into the stands and tears started coming down their faces. It's amazing. But I'd love to stay at home with my family and my dogs, sleep in my own bed, and go to a track meet nearby like the Europeans do."

The big European meets run from July through September, and there is simply no way the United States can compete. Increasingly, Masback notes, the Europeans have been encroaching on May and June, part of the season he is trying to establish on a regular basis in America. All he can really do, it appears, is work to increase track's popularity among Americans while wooing corporate sponsors, all the while hoping for a breakthrough track-and-field athlete to promote more aggressively than any has been promoted before. An athlete like Marion Jones.

"Given her age and the platform she will have, Marion has the opportunity to transcend sports and become an international icon," Masback said as he sat in a hotel lobby on the eve of the U.S. Nationals. "There have been only three athletes who have ever done that: Pelé, Muhammad Ali, and Michael Jordan. She has the chance to be the first female athlete to do that. She's the only one who has that chance. No one said to her, 'You've got to predict you're going to win five gold medals.' But that's what champions do."

But becoming the savior of track and field is not Marion's responsibility, Masback believes. Her responsibility is to her personal dreams, which, if she achieves them, would be good for the sport. "If she even begins to approach her potential and her goals," he said, "she will be a key person in helping us revive track and field in this country."

FRIDAY BROKE DARK and dreary, and though the drizzle let up occasionally, the sun didn't break through the clouds, the temperature hovered around sixty degrees, and only the most dedicated track fans—no more than five or six thousand—sat in the Hayward Field stands.

Word that Michael Johnson had withdrawn from the 200 with a leg injury after running a qualifying heat the previous day further dampened the proceedings. As the reigning Olympic champion and world record holder in the 200, Johnson's scheduled race against Maurice Greene, who had recently broken the world record in the 100, was the most anticipated matchup of the meet. Nothing seemed to be going right in Eugene.

The long jump began at 4:55 P.M. and Marion arrived at the track several hours early. Her warm-up was encouraging, particularly when the flexibility of her injured leg seemed much improved. She lay on her back, wrapped a jump rope around the ball of her right foot and pulled her leg up across her body until her injured knee touched the ground behind her shoulder. She repeated the process over and over, occasionally twisting her knee right and left as if she were daring it to fail her. Then she went over to the massage table for one last rubdown. She was as ready as she'd ever be.

Marion took the lead with her first jump. At 22-3, it was nine inches short of her winning jump in Raleigh but she was well ahead of the field. Her second jump was foul and when nobody else was close at the end of the second round, she passed on her third and fourth jumps and sat huddled in a heavy coat on a bench next to the runway where she had a good view of the action.

The wind came up and an early-evening chill descended. The competition seemed to have become frozen, too, and as many of the spectators headed home, Marion's dream scenario played itself out. She was going to win the event and defend her national championship with only two jumps. It would not be one of her greatest victories, but a win was a win. The forecast was for better weather the next two days and the 200, an event she should easily win, was coming up. In two more days, she could give her knee some rest, go to Europe where the summer track season was heating up, and start putting the final touches on her preparations for Seville.

Then lightning struck. On the fifth round, Dawn Burrell, the ninth-ranked long jumper in the world, flew through the evening gloom with an effort that needed no tape measure to elicit a response. It was clearly the best jump of the day. The small groups of remaining spectators whooped with the excitement of those whose patience has been rewarded.

"Twenty-two-ten," the public-address announcer called. "A

personal best for Dawn Burrell. Let's see if Marion Jones will pass on her next jump."

Marion got up, and, as C.J. and Trevor abandoned their seats in the bleachers to stand behind a fence closer to the action, she took off her coat and returned to the head of the runway. Concentrate. She tried to remember everything she had learned. She looked down the runway, willing her muscles to wake up after such a long rest. Twice she stared at the pit, bent over in a crouch, and launched herself toward it. But the event was over in just a few minutes. Marion's last two jumps were tentative and came up short of twenty-two feet. Cold weather, wet conditions, and aching knee notwithstanding, the number one long jumper in the world had suffered a shocking defeat.

Marion sprang up out of the pit after her final jump, hugged Dawn, and waved and smiled at the crowd. She spent the next half hour applauding the winner on the podium and taking a victory lap with Dawn and third-place finisher Shana Williams, all of whom had qualified for the World Championships.

The post–race press conference was held in a makeshift interview area in a bullpen at the edge of the track. Marion was directed to sit in the middle of the platform, directly behind the microphone, typically the winner's spot. Tom Surber, a USA Track & Field press officer, expected most of the questions would be for Marion, and he was not mistaken. Dawn Burrell sat quietly, not seeming to mind as Marion laughed and joked with reporters while a few fans stopped on their way home to listen.

"Hats off to Dawn," Marion said. "She had a wonderful performance and she definitely deserved to win. Also congratulations to uh . . ." she turned to Shana Williams helplessly and laughed at her embarrassment.

"Shana," she said. "You don't even know my name." By now,

laughter was rocketing around the bullpen, a mood that was sustained as reporters fired questions at Marion.

Marion told them that it hadn't just been cold for her, that it wasn't an excuse; Dawn and all the others had suffered through the very same conditions. She wished it had been eighty degrees and sunny, but an athlete had to be prepared for everything. And it wasn't her knee—her knee felt good.

Why take those final two jumps? a reporter asked. Why risk further injury with your spot in Seville assured?

"The competitor came out in me," she said. "I want to win. I'm not going to settle purposely for second place."

"The fact that you can't have an unbeaten season," someone asked, "Is that a big deal or not?"

"It's not a big deal any*more*," Marion said, eliciting more laughter. "Obviously, I would have loved to go through the whole season undefeated, but these things are going to happen. I've learned from it and now I'm going to move on."

Last question: "What do you have to do to improve your long jump?"

"You name it, I need to work on it."

A picture of Marion hugging Dawn appeared in the *Eugene Register-Guard* the next day, and as Marion looked at it, she spoke of how her competitive fire could transform so quickly into such good-natured acceptance of defeat.

"That was my gracious mode," she said. "Losing breaks my heart, trust me. I went back to the hotel and sulked last night. C.J. can attest to that. Many a time, my mom would have to take the chess set away from my brother and me because I was a sore loser. But I learned over the years it's important not to be a sore loser. Or if you are, don't show it. I think the true competitor comes out when you act graciously in defeat.

"Losing puts things in perspective. If you win all the time, it would be easy to believe nobody could ever beat you. Losing reminds me there's going to be somebody out there who's going to pop onto the scene one day just like I did and start winning."

MARION HAD BARELY ARRIVED at Hayward Field Saturday when she received two welcome pieces of news. The first was that the rain had stopped and the track had dried out overnight. The second was the fact that only seventeen runners were entered in the 200, which meant only one dropout was needed for the preliminary heats to be eliminated and the race to proceed directly to the semifinals. With luck, Marion would have only one race before Sunday's final instead of two.

Taking no chances, Marion began to warm up, but soon the word spread that one runner hadn't even made the trip, and the heats were canceled. With several hours to go before the semis, Marion lay down on the massage table, pulled the hood of her warm-up jacket down over her eyes and nose like a mask, folded her hands on her stomach, and took a nap.

Later that afternoon Marion's relief, and that of Trevor and C.J., was almost palpable as she ran effortlessly, felt a gentle wind at her back on the backstretch, and easily won her semifinal. Her time of 22.31 was half a second better than Nanceen Perry's second-place mark and three-tenths of a second better than Inger Miller's winning time in the second heat. She was headed toward a convincing win in Sunday's final, one that would help erase the sting of losing the long jump the day before and confirm her recovery from her knee injury.

After the race Marion sat happily in the bullpen, joking with a few reporters. "What she was looking for in Sunday's final?" one of them asked.

"I'm looking for a win," she said with a grin. "My first of the championships."

As Marion continued to catch her breath, she turned to C.J., remembering something. She thought she had felt a rock in her shoe at 110 meters, right as she was coming off the turn. C.J. thought that was odd, and a little troubling, since the smallest things could often make the difference in a sprint. "It didn't affect me," Marion said, "but it was weird." She had kept on running, feeling it all the way to the finish line.

C.J. asked her if it was still there, and she took off her right shoe and turned it over to shake out the rock.

"There it is," Marion said. "Look." C.J. took the shoe and pointed to a crack that ran through a circle half an inch in diameter slightly above the running plate that contained one of the spikes.

"It wasn't a rock," C.J. said. "It just broke."

This was more disturbing than a mere rock. How could her shoe just *break*? It could wear out, sure, but break? What if it had blown out entirely, right there in the middle of the race? The potential for disaster was very real.

The shoe, which was little more than a slender running plate attached to some gray fabric, looked like a high-tech ballet slipper. The word "Marion" was stitched in script toward the back of the upper along the side of the heel. They were new shoes, provided by Nike. The designers at the company and Marion had been working on some different plates, trying new configurations. "I guess it's back to the drawing board," Marion said.

Back under the awning, Marion met with Tobie Hatfield, a developer in Nike's advanced product-engineering department, who had given her the new shoes that very afternoon.

"I don't understand it," Hatfield said. "This is some of our strongest material."

"Has it ever happened before?" she asked.

"Only for you, Marion."

"Look at this," Trevor said, holding the shoe and shaking his head. "She only wore it once and it looks like she's been wearing it for a week. And she wasn't even running fast. What if she was going for a world record?"

In trying to make the running plate as light as possible, Hatfield explained, Nike had used a long-strand carbon fiber that requires the plate mold to be heated to a high temperature, which can make it brittle. "We had two-hundred-pound guys jumping up and down on it and we said, 'This is going to work,'" Hatfield said. "But she smoked it the first time out. She just generates so much force."

Microanalysis at a lab in Minnesota the following week would indicate that the shoe broke as Marion was negotiating the turn about halfway through the race. The centrifugal force she had created simply tore the plate apart. Particularly aggravating to Hatfield was the fact that Marion had tested the new shoe when she had returned to the track for practice the previous week. But her knee injury had kept her from generating her usual power, which might have exposed the flaw.

"Now I don't want you to feel bad," Marion said. And she began telling him what she *liked* about the shoe. The lightweight upper was fine and the arch support was excellent. And besides, she'd won the race, hadn't she?

"I'm happy because she stuck to the game plan," Trevor said of her easy victory. "She covered the field in sixty meters and then shut it down. None of that tomorrow, though. It's time for her to go for it. As fast as she can. Don't worry about the knee. Don't worry about anything. All out. Marion Jones. Bang!"

• • •

MARION EASILY DEFENDED her national championship at 200 meters on Sunday. The people in the crowd
whooped as the staggered start allowed them to see how easily she
was overtaking the other runners, and as she came out of the
curve she was well in front. Marion in full flight was something to
see: her legs, so long compared to the others, reached out and
grabbed the track, taking more and more relative to the others
with each stride. Her face was loose, even relaxed—the only part
of her body not enlisted in the effort to move faster.

Marion's time, 22.10, placed her well ahead of the second-place
finisher, collegian Latasha Jenkins, who finished in 22.36. Inger
Miller was third in 22.46. It had been a nice, quiet, drama-free
victory at last.

Making the afternoon even sweeter, C.J. got off a fine series of
throws—three of them beyond seventy feet—to finish second to
John Godina, the top-ranked shot-putter in the world, and make
the team going to Seville. She could go after her four gold medals
and he could go after his one, Marion joked in the media bullpen.
"That's our goal. I say it a little more than he does, though."

She was still going for four, then? a reporter asked.

"You mean, have my goals changed because I was second in the
long jump?" she said. "No, they haven't. If anything, they've been
put into stone."

Trevor asked her if she felt any problems with her knee during
the race, and she said she couldn't remember. She thought that
was good. If she couldn't remember it, it must have been fine.

Marion left the track, returned to the hotel, and packed for Europe, where the summer track season was about to begin. For the
first time all week, the sun was shining.

# 8

*A* leaky mist hung over Paul Derr Field. The precipitation never reached a level that could properly be called rain, but rain gear was the uniform of the day and the track acquired a light covering of moisture that neither increased into puddles nor decreased enough to show any dry patches. The grayness of the sky didn't diminish, either, as Marion continued training.

Wearing a slicker and sweatpants between drills, and huddling inside the shed with her teammates during breaks, her mood was like the weather. Not bad, nothing to be upset about, but not bright and sunny, either.

Two days after the U.S. Nationals in Eugene, Marion ran the 200 in a meet in Oslo that marked the beginning of the 1999 Golden League competition. She won easily with a time of 22.13, making her chances for a share of the million-dollar bonus look stronger than ever. A week later, at a meet in Rome, she won again with a 22.18 clocking. In between, she ran the 100 in Lausanne in 10.80, the world's fastest time in the season to date. But she was not totally satisfied.

"Everybody was saying I looked great," she said, "but I didn't feel sharp, sharp, sharp. And my times weren't the best. My knee has been a little tender after races, but some massage and ice, and it's fine. Sometimes, it's a little stiff when it rains, but when I'm training and competing I don't feel anything."

There was, she noted, a dilemma about how to proceed. When she was competing in Europe, she longed to come home and do nothing but train. She could go through her drills, totally rehabilitate her knee and get her sharpness back. But going months at a time with no competition was out of the question. Whether she was at her peak of conditioning or not, she had to race. She had to get in the blocks alongside the best in the world. She had to feel her confidence build as the World Championships approached. And besides, she had been winning her races by large margins—almost half a second in some of the 200s. If her times weren't the best, some suggested, perhaps her competitors bore some of the responsibility.

That was one excuse she would not accept. When she set her personal bests in the sprints in South Africa the previous September, nobody was close to her. When Florence Griffith Joyner set her world records, she was alone on the track. Competition is nice, and she had always responded well to it, but the person responsible for Marion's times is Marion, and nobody else.

MARION'S DOMINATION OF the sprints was a blessing in one respect. It meant she and Trevor could turn their full attention to the long jump. Her running schedule overseas had not left much time for practice, but now they were back home, and, with no distractions, the long jump would have their full attention. "Every day this week, we're going to do something different in the long jump," Trevor said. "We're going to get it right."

To Marion, it all seemed so simple. She didn't begin competing in the event until her senior year in high school, had little chance to make any progress while at college, and only now was getting the sustained opportunity to develop her skills.

"Most of the people I jump against, that's all they do," she said. "People say I don't jump like Jackie, I don't jump like Heike Drechsler. But they've been doing it their whole lives. And Trevor has never coached a long jumper before, so he's still learning along with me."

Between the two of them, they broke it down.

Approach: head down, body angled forward—the drive phase all over again as she raced the length of the approach strip. Technique in the air: arms back, chin up, reach out as if she is opening a door, one knee up and then the other as her legs come through. Landing: stretch with the legs, bring both arms through hard—hard!—fall forward. And, perhaps most important of all: knowledge of where she is on the runway, how fast she is running, where she will be at takeoff.

Trevor places a mark thirteen steps from the board that Marion tries to hit with her right leg. "My number-one goal as I move down the runway is to hit it just right so I can attack the board," she said. "If I don't, I'm going to have to stutter step, go pitty-pat. That's no good. Running is my strength and I've got to take advantage of it."

Over and over again, Marion crouches low and springs down the runway, building speed, running so fast it seems that she'll just run through the pit and keep going. But at the last moment she hits the board and leaps into the air. Her back arches and her body, so powerful and contained when she's running, stretches out and opens up to the air and the sand. Trevor watches from the end of the pit, his arms crossed, leaning against a rake. Each time Marion lands in the pit she sighs, bounds up, and trots back up the runway.

One thing Marion has not lacked in the long jump is advice. Almost everyone in track and field, it seems, knows what the problem is, and how to fix it. Devote one entire off-season to jumping, for instance. For Marion, that's impossible, since the sprints are her premier events and require most of her attention.

Others suggest that she give up the long jump entirely and concentrate on the sprints. But that sort of talk only goads her into sticking with the event: "It just makes me want to come out here and jump, jump, jump and prove them all wrong," she said.

But the most often-heard criticism was the one that bothered her the most: She needed a new coach.

"I don't need to ask for help," Marion said. "We understand what the problem is. I just need to dedicate more time to it. Slowly, with every practice, we're putting more in and one day we'll have it all down. And when we do, we'll be the ones who have done it—me and Trevor."

Touched by Marion's confidence in him, Trevor was alternately amused and irritated by those who thought she needed outside assistance. When she didn't make the long-jump finals in the World Championships in Athens in 1997, nobody wanted to coach her then, he noted. But the next year, when she became the top long jumper in the world, suddenly she needed a new coach.

"She's still learning," Trevor said. "People have to understand that. But one day she's going to have it all down and you know what's going to happen then? She's going to put the record so far out there, her kids won't be able to break it."

After practicing the long jump all week, Marion returned to competition—against Chandra Sturrup for the championship of Paul Derr Field. Trevor planted a small American flag in the sand to mark Marion's jumps, then found a banner left from the June high school meet, when Marion injured her knee in the very same sandpit.

"It's the national flag of the Bahamas," Trevor teased Chandra, who scowled, watched Marion's next jump, then took her own turn.

At practice Marion and Chandra do almost everything together. When they can conduct an exercise at the same time, they do so with military precision. One drill requires them to stand on either side of a hurdle, facing the same direction. They lift their inside legs up and over the hurdle, skip forward a meter or so on the opposite leg to the next hurdle, and repeat the process until they've cleared all ten hurdles. They do this together fluidly, and without stopping. Their legs come over the hurdle and they bring them down together with one distinctive sound. *Thump, thump, thump,* all the way to the end.

The two running partners don't talk much. After practice they are friendly with each other, even warm. But when they are between drills, they often rest at different spots on the track. They are all business. Trevor doesn't hover over them, making sure they do the work. It's apparent that he told them what to do hours ago and sees no reason to check up. They are professionals, and they will do the work.

Shortly before Marion was to fly to Paris for the resumption of her European season, she and Chandra went through one final workout—drill after drill, sprint after sprint, long jump after long jump until they were spent. The clouds were gone now and, as the temperature climbed well into the nineties, the two women approached the limits of exhaustion.

"They hate me about now," Trevor said as the session wound down. "I destroyed them this week. But this is the only week off we have between now and the World Championships and we got a lot of good work done." As she came off the track, Marion wasn't feeling well, and instead of hanging around to cool down and chat with her teammates, she got into her jeep and drove home.

Several days later, in Paris, she won her eighteenth straight victory at 200 meters in 21.99, becoming the first woman in 1999 to break 22 seconds.

ON JULY 10 Marion and C.J. fired up the barbecue, turned on the television set, and watched the U.S. women's soccer team—which contained so many former University of North Carolina athletes—beat China to win the Women's World Cup. In Europe, where they had felt lucky to see the United States win its semifinal game on television a few days earlier, they had stayed up cheering until 3 A.M. and now they were shouting again. But it wasn't only the victory that excited Marion, it was also what it represented.

"The fact you can get ninety thousand people to come see a women's game," Marion said of the crowd in the Rose Bowl. "It's difficult to say now what statement it really makes, but I have a feeling we're going to look back in a couple of years and say things changed a lot after the women's soccer team beat China."

It has so much to do with attitudes, she said, with perceptions and traditional ideas of what women can do and should do. There is a lot of progress to be made, but so much has been accomplished already. Women's professional basketball has been firmly established in the United States for the first time. The college game has reached new heights of popularity. And now there is a boom in women's soccer no one could have foreseen.

But Marion saw more than triumph in the soccer team's victory; she saw the potential pitfalls that accompanied it, too.

"I'm Mia Hamm's biggest fan simply because she could stay so mentally tough through all of it," she said. "She didn't score in a couple of games and everybody was asking her, 'Mia, what's wrong?' I could see myself in that situation—people saying I didn't have a great start even when I win, or wondering what's the matter with the long jump. I just hope I can handle it as well as she did if it happens to me."

John Capriotti of Nike is one of those betting it will happen soon.

"If I taught a sports-marketing class on who to look for, I would use a Marion Jones model," Capriotti said as he discussed the company's intricately planned international advertising campaign leading into the Olympics. "A great athlete, a great-looking woman with a great personality who speaks very well. She's the total package. I've never seen this much interest at Nike in any athlete except Michael Jordan. Everybody in the company wants her for photo shoots and appearances, but we have to be really careful how we use her because she's got to have time to train. I insist on that."

Marion was amused by the early indications of what fame extending beyond track and field might be like. Oakley sunglasses mounted a magazine and billboard campaign in which her expression was so serious she could barely recognize herself. The two-page photograph of her coming out of the starting blocks in Annie Leibovitz's book *Women,* which was published late in 1999, made her look as if she were ready to go to war. Peter Lindbergh's photos for TAG Heuer watches were certainly glamorous, but the first thing she thought when she saw them was, "You would *never* see me walking down the street in a tube top like that."

It was exciting to see her face in a fashion magazine, she thought, but at the same time it seemed not quite real. "It's kind of a facade," she said, "not the real Marion. I would hope people recognize me more for what I do on the track than for an advertisement in *Vogue.*"

Occasionally Marion will read that she may turn out to be track and field's standard-bearer during the coming decade— that she, more than any man, will be the one who raises her sport's visibility in the United States. Her performances and personality are the key to this, of course, but Marion recognizes there is another aspect as well: simple good fortune.

"It would mean that I came along at the perfect time," she said of how the explosion in collegiate and women's sports has expanded opportunities for young women everywhere. "It would mean that I'm a woman of the new millennium."

# 9

*T*he contrast between the World Track and Field Championships and the U.S. Nationals could not have been more stark. The ancient Spanish city of Seville, broiling under a cloudless sky, and the rain and chill of Oregon, were two months, one continent, and an ocean apart. And compared with the low profile of the American meet, signs of the international competition were apparent around every corner in Seville.

Battalions of police patrolled every entrance to the Estadio Olympico in pairs. An army of young people in orange T-shirts met visitors at the airport and throughout the city to solve problems, give directions, and answer questions before they were asked. Fleets of large buses stood ready to whisk athletes, coaches, officials, and reporters to and from more than a dozen hotels all over town. The planning and organization had been painstaking, worthy of an Olympics, and unthinkable at a track meet anywhere in the United States.

Marion and C.J. saw the grimly serious nature of the business

at hand when they attended a U.S. team meeting two nights before the meet began and heard a report on a technical meeting a
day earlier. It was like a war, they were told, as the various countries vied for the best lanes, the most desirable starting times, and
any other advantages they could obtain.

"It was very coldhearted," said one official who had attended
many such meetings in the past. "I remember when people respected and liked the U.S. team. It's not like that anymore. Watch
your back." To guard against incidents, the U.S. team hired a
squad of private police who traveled with them at all times.

MARION HAD PERFORMED well in the European
meets leading up to the World Championships, winning the 100
in London, and the 200 in four other meets to stay on track for
the Golden League jackpot. She now had the two fastest times of
the year in the 100, as well as the four fastest in the 200, and seven
of the top eight. Her domination of the 200 was so great, and her
victory in the Worlds so likely, that after finishing a poor fifth at
a meet in Paris, Christine Arron announced she would not run
the event in Seville but would try her luck in the 100. Arron's
chances there didn't look much better; she had run under 11 seconds only once all year, 10.97 at an earlier Paris meet.

If there was one straw of encouragement Marion's rivals could
grasp, it was the fact that Marion had not set a personal best in either event in 1999. But the more she thought about it, the less
concerned she felt. She was winning easily, and she was doing it
without being forced to extend herself prior to the World Championships. The best was yet to come.

It was too bad she couldn't see her face coming down the
straightaway of the races she was winning, C.J. told her. She

looked so relaxed. If she had gum in her mouth she could blow a bubble, he said. The other runners were so intense by comparison. "I'm winning without taking much out of my body," Marion said. "It's a good sign. I'm totally and completely confident."

The long jump was another matter. Marion had lost her one competition since the U.S. Nationals in the event, again to Heike Drechsler in Linz, Austria, and once more she had gone back to the drawing board. She and Trevor were both frustrated, she said, because she was much more tense on the runway than in 1998 when she was so far ahead of the other jumpers. Her face and arms in particular seemed rigid and she could feel herself chopping off her final steps to the board. Relax, she kept reminding herself. Just relax.

One hopeful sign was the fact that none of the other top women in the world were jumping consistently well either. Maureen Maggi of Brazil had leaped 23-10 in the altitude of Bogotá earlier in the year, but otherwise only Italy's Fiona May, with a jump of 23-0½, and Niurka Montalvo of Spain, who had set a national record, 23-0¾, on August 10, had gone over 23 feet all year. Another stroke of good fortune was the fact that Heike Drechsler had withdrawn with a calf injury. If Marion could get off a decent jump, nothing spectacular, she might win the event yet.

True to their plan, Trevor had put Marion through a full long-jump workout almost every day that she wasn't competing since she had returned to Europe: takeoffs, full-speed approaches, landings, the works. Sometimes she jumped as often as a dozen times a day. "I've jumped, jumped, jumped, and I've run, run, run," Marion said. "At least I know one thing. My knee is fine."

The one change Marion was prepared to make in her schedule was in the relay. For the first time in public, at a Nike-sponsored press conference, she gave herself some wiggle room concerning the 4×400. After her three individual events, she said, Trevor would assess her physical condition and determine if she was ready to run the 400 meters. "If he doesn't feel he wants to have me go through that stress," she said, "then I'm just going to run the four by one."

One glance at the schedule of events illustrated the problem. It was one thing to talk about competing eleven times on eight different days during a nine-day meet, but it was something else to confront the reality of how it would be done.

On the first two days, Marion would compete five times in the long jump and the 100. The long-jump qualifying round, in fact, had originally been scheduled at 10:30 A.M. on Saturday, the meet's opening day, fifteen minutes before the first heat of the dash. Would she have to run back and forth across the track between events and jump shortly after running 100 meters? Or perhaps she would even have to skip a jump altogether. Fortunately, the schedule was adjusted. The heats in the 100 would begin at 10:45 and Marion would run in the first one. The long-jump qualifying round would start an hour later, and the second round of the 100 would be run in the evening.

Nor did the pace slacken after that. The semifinals and final of the 100 were on Sunday and the long-jump final was on Monday. Three days into the meet and her two most challenging events would be behind her. By contrast, the 200 took place over a leisurely four-day span. So there would be plenty of time to make a final decision on the relays, which came last.

Marion was excited and relieved that at last the moment was at hand. There was further satisfaction in the fact that C.J. had also been performing at a high level during the summer. He now had the second and third best throws of the year, and hopes of giving John Godina and the others a run for the gold. The trials and finals of the shot put would be contested on Saturday, too. The opening day of the World Championships was going to be busy.

SEVILLE'S ESTADIO OLYMPICO had been inaugurated several years earlier, but in the days leading up to the meet it seemed still under construction—all freshly poured cement and wire cables waiting to be connected. With a capacity of sixty thousand spectators, the stadium had a graceful deck at the top that extended over the seating areas and kept most of the spectators in the shade much of the time. The athletes might toil in the sun for nine days, but the paying customers would be largely spared.

Taken strictly as a track meet, the World Championships are considered by the sport's aficionados to be better than the Olympics, if only because there is no stage to share with gymnasts, swimmers, basketball players, and the like. In the years since the meet was inaugurated in Helsinki in 1983, it had become such a huge enterprise that nations tried to outbid each other for the event. The 1997 championships in Athens were held shortly before the 2004 Olympics were to be awarded, and Greek sports officials, in the fight for the Olympics and worried about the signal empty seats might send to International Olympic Committee members, distributed free tickets. Athens got the Games.

In Seville, there was a similar problem that dismayed the organizers: The stadium was often less than half full. Perhaps this was because the heat had driven too many of the city's residents to the beach. Or maybe it was an indication that track and field, steadily losing fans to European soccer, is in decline.

The championships were brought to fruition by Primo Nebiolo, the redoubtable president of the International Amateur Athletic Federation, who, in less than two decades, took the organization from an annual budget of $50,000 and digs in a down-and-out London neighborhood to a $50 million enterprise with offices in Monte Carlo. The meet had the enormous good fortune of coming along at the same time a free market arose in track and field, a sport that for generations had pretended it was a home only for amateurs. Winners of gold medals at the championships receive sixty thousand dollars, as opposed to Olympic champions who compete only for glory—and bonuses from their shoe companies.

The meet's standing was also helped when Carl Lewis made his international debut and won three gold medals at the first championship, and again when Mike Powell broke Bob Beamon's 23-year-old long-jump record eight years later in Tokyo. Soon the event itself was on the fast track as its four-year cycle was compressed into biennial status. No World Championships have ever been held in the United States, and, though Stanford University has bid twice, the lack of interest in track in the U.S. bars hope for the foreseeable future.

THE NIGHT MARION and C.J. arrived in Seville, they fell asleep early and were awakened by a knock at the door. It was Trevor. "Did you hear?" he said. "Merlene's been busted."

A groggy C.J. relayed the news to Marion, who, barely awake, mumbled, "Yeah?" and fell back asleep. The next morning, when she was able to process the news, she turned on the television to see if it could possibly be true. It was.

Merlene Ottey had tested positive for using the banned steroid nandrolone at a meet in Lucerne on July 5. Though the great Jamaican sprinter passionately denied any wrongdoing, she was out of the meet and her career might very well be over. This was, an IAAF official said, the last thing track and field needed before the opening of the World Championships.

In the weeks leading up to the meet, the sport had suffered one drug-related blow after another. Javier Sotomayor, the Cuban high jumper who held the world record, had tested positive for cocaine at the Pan-American Games in Vancouver. Former Olympic sprint champion Linford Christie had tested positive for the same steroid as Ottey. And U.S. sprint star Dennis Mitchell's appeal of a two-year suspension for using testosterone had been denied.

At thirty-nine, Ottey was still running excellent times, and, over the years, she had won fourteen medals in the World Championships, more than any other athlete. She was also the last person to beat Marion in a foot race, winning the 100 meters in a meet in Japan at the end of the 1997 season. Marion, who had always appreciated Merlene's poise in public and graciousness to her, was stunned.

"Was she a role model to you?" a reporter asked.

"She still is," Marion replied.

She couldn't say Merlene was innocent, Marion said, after having some time to reflect. But it certainly seemed odd that so many tests were coming up positive all of a sudden. Had there been a change they didn't know about? Were the tests themselves ever investigated? It all got back to the original problem: the lack of a test everyone could trust. Until one came along, the athletes would remain suspicious and disheartened.

Most distressing of all was the fact that on the eve of track and field's great international showcase, the major topic of conversation was drugs. "In the past couple of weeks," Marion told a gathering at a heavily attended Nike press conference on the banks of the Guadalquivir River, "our beautiful and lovely sport has been marred."

THE DAY BEFORE THE meet began, Christine Arron held court at a press conference arranged by her sporting goods sponsor, Reebok, and American reporters were given their first real opportunity to ask her about Marion directly. She did not disappoint them. Sitting behind a table next to an interpreter, Arron was a striking figure, her coppery skin set off by short tight curls that gleamed an impossibly iridescent yellow. She had been aiming for purple, she said, but her dye had failed.

"I think she's more beatable this year," Arron said of Marion in response to a question by Philip Hersh of the *Chicago Tribune*, who led the media charge. "She hasn't made a lot of improvement in her times. I don't see that she's making much progress. Maybe she's training the way I am and the results don't always show up on the track."

What about being quoted in *L'Equipe*, the French newspaper, saying that she considered Marion arrogant? Hersh asked. She couldn't recall using that word in talking to the French sports newspaper, Arron said, but she would be happy to use it now. She had tried to congratulate Marion after a race and had been brushed off, she said. That was certainly arrogant. She disapproved of the way American athletes promote themselves. And surely, talk of winning four gold medals is a bit much.

When, inevitably, the subject turned to drugs and Merlene Ottey's suspension, Arron said France was leading the way by using blood tests, and other countries should follow suit. She was certain there were many more cheaters in track and field than those who had been caught. Why, there are athletes who travel from meet to meet all over the world and perform well without the proper rest and recovery period. She had her doubts about how that could be done.

Reportorial antennae pricked up around the room as the English translation was read. Athletes who travel all over the world? She couldn't possibly mean . . . But no. As the interpreter read the rest of Arron's lengthy remarks from shorthand notes, there was also a reference to athletes who had set world records on drugs. Her grievance was general, not specific. And, to her credit, Arron answered at length and without rancor when asked about suggestions that in order to have burst onto the scene so spectacularly in 1998 perhaps *she* had been using drugs.

Later, in her hotel room, Marion was amused by the fuss.

"There are several women I compete against who should be getting more recognition than they are and everybody's concerned about Christine, who really hasn't done anything this year," she said. "You've got Inger Miller who's running 22.1s and 22.2s. You have Sevatheda Fynes. You have all these other women who are going at it head to head with me every week and not backing down. But it's all Christine. I don't understand it. It's funny."

MARION BEGAN HER first day of competition smartly. Feeling loose and comfortable in the early morning heat, she easily won her first round of the 100, finishing several steps ahead of her closest pursuer in a nice relaxed time, 11.22. What a fast track, she thought. Good things are going to happen here. Up in the stands, Trevor was equally pleased. "We've got a long day ahead of us," he said.

Across the track at the long-jump pit, Fiona May quickly made a statement, jumping 23-1¼, her best of the season, on her first try in the qualifying round. Marion's opening effort, 21-9, was short of the 22-3¾ needed to make the finals automatically.

"She's slowing down on the runway," Trevor said from his nearby seat in the stands, and he motioned to Marion, who shrugged as if to say, "I know."

Half an hour later, she got off the third best jump of the day, 22-4¼, good enough to qualify, and to raise her hopes for the final on Monday evening. She felt more comfortable coming down the runway than she had all year, and her form had held up nicely in the air. The landings could have been better, she thought, but what else is new? On her way back to the hotel to rest before the second round of the 100, Marion was deep in conversation with Trevor about whether she should move a step back on the runway. The long jump was still very much a work in progress.

In the evening, the pace in the 100 picked up. Ekaterini Thanou of Greece got things rolling by winning the first heat in 10.86. Inger Miller danced jubilantly off the track after winning the second heat in the same time, her personal best. Christine Arron won the third heat in 11 seconds flat, and then it was Marion's turn.

Marion approached the blocks in her customary way, each movement a habit. She stretched, she bounced, she massaged her legs, she stared at the finish line. She took deep breaths, and never looked at the other runners. She crouched down and eased herself into the blocks. She lowered her head in concentration.

She false started.

Uh-oh, she thought. That computerized starting gun again. Remember what happened to Merlene in Athens? Pay attention.

Off safely the second time, Marion led from the start, extending her lead with each long stride and sneaking a glance at the clock as she crossed the line: 10.76, a record for the World Championships and the fastest time in the world in 1999. After slowing to a stop, she clapped her hands twice, gave herself a quick thumbs up, and trotted back up the track. "I sat back and watched Inger and the other girls run great races and I decided to join the club," Marion told the press, and once again she raved about the speed of the track. "It's only going to be faster tomorrow."

For Trevor, the best news was not on the clock but in Marion's stride. Without extending herself, she had once again hit that 10.76 mark he had predicted to such amazement two years before. Only four other women in history had ever run faster. The outlook for Sunday couldn't have been better.

Marion then climbed the stadium stairs and sat in the stands to watch C.J. compete in the shot put.

After taking the lead on his first attempt, C.J. fell to fifth early in the fourth round, and when his own throw, which appeared to contend for the lead, was negated by a questionable foul call, he seemed out of the running. John Godina, the world's top shotputter, was also having problems, so a golden opportunity was getting away from C.J. Marion watched intently, yelling encouragement when C.J. approached the launch area, then sitting back in silence after each throw. On his fifth attempt C.J. got off a good effort, moving into second place, thirteen inches behind Oliver Sven-Buder of Germany.

As C.J. stepped into the launch circle for his final attempt,

Marion was struck by a single thought: He was going to win. All the work, all the energy, all the days he had returned home from practice so exhausted he could hardly move were going to pay off. She had sensed it at home when she saw how much effort he was giving to his goal of winning a gold medal, and she could sense it now.

C.J. was intensely focused as he prepared for his next throw, frowning. Chalk colored the junction of his neck and powerful shoulder, where he had been cradling the shot all day. He wore a torn gray T-shirt under his uniform, a workingman's shirt. He moved deliberately toward the circle, wasting no movement, saving it all for the moment of the throw when he would propel his body around the seven-foot circle with remarkable agility and grace for someone so big, building momentum until he reached the precipice, and then letting all that energy flow into his arm, through his palm, and into the shot. An explosion of muscle.

Needing a personal best to win, he told himself he had nothing to lose, that he should throw as hard as he possibly could. If he was ever going to face an all-or-nothing situation, this was it. He shifted the shot from one hand to the other, chalking it. He looked out toward the field, broken by white lines of tape marking the distances, and then turned his back. He nestled the shot against the chin and, with no hestitation, bent low and began to spin. He flung his body twice around the circle, leaping nimbly from one foot to the other, and let fly with his customary shout. The shot arced high and kept climbing, farther and farther. While it was still in the air he gave another bellow, louder this time, an unprecedented display for him. He knew where that shot was going. It landed on a strip of tape measuring an arc of twenty-two meters, a tape that had not been hit all evening. It moved him into first place and erased all of C.J.'s normal impassiveness in an instant.

He screamed again, bent his head way back, and thrust both fists skyward in triumph. Twice more he bellowed and beat his chest, a celebration of his first great international triumph, which had come on a throw of 71-6, more than a foot beyond his previous personal best.

After watching Sven-Buder fail to match the distance on his final throw, the enormity of what had happened began to sink in. "I haven't won a world championship before," C.J. said later, smiling and shaking his head. "It's nice to do what you have to do when you have to do it."

Marion was on her feet shouting, both arms pumping the air above her head, and then she turned to hug Trevor. She gestured to the track, and C.J., beaming, turned and pointed to her, blowing kisses.

"It was all I could do to keep from jumping over that railing and giving him a huge hug and kiss and telling him how proud I was of him and how much I loved him," said Marion, thrilled that at last C.J. would receive the recognition he had deserved for so long. After a lengthy celebration, she sat down and contemplated the moment, her head straight ahead, her face stoic. Only a few small tears betrayed any emotion now.

A few minutes later, the man who said the last thing he wanted was visibility, who so disliked being in the public eye, who would rather go to the dentist than speak in public, turned into a seasoned media veteran. In the hothouse atmosphere of the mixed zone, where the athletes run a gauntlet of media standing on the other side of a long, low fence, C.J. went from one TV camera to another, grazed the radio microphones, wandered down to where the writers stood, and then went into the interview room and un-burdened himself.

"Other than the birth of my kids and my marriage to Marion, this is the happiest day of my life," said C.J., who would spend the next four days at the stadium signing autographs and posing for pictures. "When you spend an entire year preparing for six throws, it's all about being satisfied with your performance. It's great to live up to my potential."

Marion sat on a ledge signing autographs and happily observing C.J.'s debut as a public figure. To the television reporters who asked for a comment, she said, "No, this is C.J.'s moment. Let him tell you about it."

Soon it was time for her to return to the hotel to rest for Sunday's semifinals and final of the 100 meters, so for once it was C.J. who stayed behind to celebrate a victory. And before the competition began the following evening, it was C.J. who became the first American athlete at the 1999 World Championships to hear the national anthem played in his honor.

INGER MILLER WAS on a roll. Her winning time in Sunday evening's first 100-meter semifinal was 10.80. In twenty-four hours, she had lowered her personal best twice and she looked fierce on the track, supremely confident. She had twice fought off some of the fastest women in the world and looked smooth doing it. Her form was nearly perfect, and she was so relaxed that she even seemed to close her eyes a few times during the race.

Watching on television in a room near the practice track inside the stadium, Marion was impressed. The track was not the only thing that was fast in Seville. The competition was heating up, too. Better drop a fast time, she thought, as she lined up for her own semifinal a few minutes later. Just to let everybody know you're still here. It wouldn't be good to have your competitors thinking they have an edge going into the final.

For the second day in a row, she false started.

This is getting old, she thought. One more and you won't be *in* the final. Gail Devers, the two-time Olympic champion, was next to her on the right. Zhanna Pintusevich, her old friend from the 1997 World Championships, had one of the inside lanes. She had to be careful at the start, and yet she couldn't give anyone a step. She positioned herself slowly this time and waited until she was sure the gun had gone off. Gail and Zhanna got off fast, and at first Marion slipped slightly behind. Still, she stuck with her drive phase, keeping her head down a few steps longer than the others, picking up speed with every step until she pulled ahead around the thirty-meter mark. By the midway point she was decisively ahead. She crossed the line in 10.83, with Gail and Zhanna a step behind. A good race; she'd held her form. Not as fast as Inger, but that was fine. She'd be ready for the final.

With an hour and forty-five minutes to wait before the 9 P.M. start, Marion and Chandra Sturrup, who had also made the final, began the uphill walk from the track to a stadium tunnel leading to an inside warm-up track. There they saw C.J. standing next to an ambulance and motioning to them to get in. Why walk a quarter mile before the biggest race of the year when a friendly ambulance driver was more than happy to give you a ride?

Inside the stadium, there was nothing to do but wait. Already warmed up, and with no need to jog or stretch, Marion lay down on Steve Bernabeu's table, stared straight ahead, and composed herself. It was the first time her chiropractor had seen her steely, unblinking pre-race gaze, and though he wondered if there were a problem, he decided not to ask. Just my game face, Marion told him later, and they both laughed.

As she considered how fast so many of the runners had been in the early heats, Marion realized their confidence level must be rising. They must truly believe they had a chance to beat her for the first time in nearly two years, she thought. But she, too, felt relaxed, smooth, comfortable. She had dropped a 10.76 with ease and she was ready to run faster. Were they? At eight-thirty, the call came. Time to go out on the track. No ambulance this time.

As the starting time approached, a sweet breeze swept through the stadium, and the last rays of sun crawled up the highest rows of seats in the east stands. The arena was no more than a quarter full as the premier events of the evening approached, the finals of the men's and women's 100-meters. The two races were scheduled ten minutes apart. Ladies first.

At eight minutes to nine, without announcement or ceremony, the runners appeared on the track wearing T-shirts and long pants over their uniforms and tossing their bags in front of the tall boxes behind the starting blocks that announced the lane numbers. Some sat and stretched. Others jogged or sprinted down the track. Gail Devers sat at the fifty-meter mark and massaged her leg.

Marion sprinted down the track, then returned and sat on a box that displayed the number five. Gail would be running to her left, Ekaterini Thanou to her right. The runners packed away their warm-up clothes and changed into their spikes while several TV cameras invaded the space directly in front of them. As the name, country, and a brief description of career highlights were read and translated, a cameraman walked up, and a huge close-up of each runner, not so alone with her private thoughts, filled the large television screens in two corners of the stadium. The announcer took his time, oblivious to the nervous energy on the track.

"In lane five, representing the USA," the announcement came, "the defending champion and 1997 World Championships gold medalist, Marion Jones!" The camera zoomed in on Marion. Her hair was pulled back in a short, tight ponytail. Her eyes were closed.

The runners approached the blocks. Marion jumped up and down three times and then rocked her torso from one side to the other. She stared placidly at the finish line, took in a big breath, and blew it out. She bent forward from her waist, letting her arms hang loosely, dangling her fingers just an inch above the track. She jiggled both legs quickly, shaking them while keeping her feet in place. She blew out another breath. She gave her legs a quick massage by pounding them with her fists. This was her ritual, as habitual as her preparation for a free throw.

She crouched and stuck her feet in the blocks. Her starts in the previous rounds had been so good, she thought. Now it was time to really nail one. Get out in front early and the others will be demoralized. They all knew she was the one to beat and that nobody catches her from behind.

The starter called the runners to the blocks. They assumed their crouches. The gun went up. Marion lowered her head, controlling her breath.

False start. Inger Miller this time. The runners jogged several meters down the track, then returned to the start. Regroup, Marion told herself. Be loose. Be comfortable. Be ready to fly.

Marion stuck her feet back in the blocks and carefully placed her fingers on the track before her. This time, when she looked down the track her face was quizzical, expectant. Her forehead wrinkled and her eyes opened wide for an instant. The expression disappeared, and she slowly lowered her head. The gun went up again. "*Listos . . .*"

She nailed the start. Really nailed it. Even the fact that she might have popped up just a bit at the sound of the gun didn't matter. This is the best of the four, she thought, and, as she came out of the blocks, she could tell the race was hers. By the second step, she knew she was in the lead. It was that feeling of perfect order again, one she would not relinquish. "I never looked back from there," she said. "I felt so powerful, my stride felt so smooth. No one was going to catch me."

And no one did. Increasing her lead with virtually every step, Marion had a feeling approaching invincibility. Unlike 1997, when she could feel Zhanna Pintusevich closing in at the end, there was no one with her this time. For an athlete, it was the ultimate reward: total domination of a World Championship event. They had all been running so fast the last two days, she thought. How fast must she be running now?

At the end, the excitement overwhelmed her. Two steps from the finish line, she raised her arms in triumph. So fierce and intent for 100 meters, a smile shot across her face the instant she crossed the line. Trevor and C.J. thought her exuberance may have cost her a few hundredths of a second, maybe even a personal best. Marion didn't care. She had been so excited she hadn't even thought about it. What a great race it was, and she had won her first gold medal. "I don't regret it at all," she said.

Marion's time, 10.70, was the fifth fastest in history; only she and Florence Griffith Joyner had ever run faster. Meet officials replayed the race over and over again on the stadium's screens, and the crowd yelled, "Mah-Ree-Yone!" in tribute.

She walked back up the track, smiling and waving, stood at the fifty-meter mark and waved some more. Finally the runners in the men's final came out for their warm-ups, and, waving all the while, the fastest woman in the world made her way into the mixed zone to kiss her husband and talk to the press.

WHAT A STRUGGLE it had been for Inger Miller, a struggle dating back to high school. She had faced Marion in ten races over 100 and 200 meters in 1999, and numerous other times the previous two years, but her only victories remained those two races in the Arcadia Invitational during Marion's freshman year in high school. Now Inger had improved her personal best in the 100 three times over a two-day period, to 10.79, and she had still finished nearly a tenth of a second behind Marion.

Ekaterini Thanou was third in 10.84, another fine time, while Zhanna Pintusevich and Gail Devers were fourth and fifth at 10.95. Christine Arron, still waiting for the results of her training to show up on the track, was sixth in 10.97. Runner for runner, it was the fastest race in history: the first time six women had bettered eleven seconds at one time.

"Disappointed?" Inger told a friend in the mixed zone. "No, I'm not disappointed. Three PRs, what can I say?" Then she grinned, shook her head, and said, "Shoot."

Three hours after C.J. had stood atop the victory stand, Marion climbed up and listened to the national anthem. When it was over, International Olympic Committee president Juan Antonio Samaranch, accompanied by Primo Nebiolo, the IAAF president, walked up and hung the gold medal around her neck.

Whoa, Marion thought. Both of them. I must be getting somewhere. Her little-girl smile, shown on the huge stadium screens, left no doubt about what she was thinking: "This is so neat."

ON MONDAY, AN HOUR before the long-jump final was due to start, a piece of skin came off Marion's little toe. Though she was happy with the shoes Nike had provided, a new upper attached to her old running plate, the major changes had been put on hold. It was the heat and the hard track at the stadium and the practice field that had caused blisters to form. The removal of a Band-Aid took skin with it and Marion winced in pain.

Steve Bernabeu and Norman Levin, an internist and rheumatologist from Virginia who had joined her medical team, discussed home-remedy foot plasters they could concoct. But for now she would have to settle for a procaine salve and hang tough. I'll be all right, she said. It won't bother me. And it didn't. After an opening jump of 22-3¾, she was in third place, trailing Fiona May by five inches and Niurka Montalvo of Spain by a fraction.

By the end of the third round, when the field was cut from twelve to eight, May had extended her distance to 22-9¾, mediocre at best for a world championship. In recent years, dozens of women had jumped farther hundreds of times. The gold medal was there for anyone who could get off one decent jump.

Still exhilarated from the night before, Marion felt fast on the runway and she exchanged a few words with Trevor between jumps. Chin down, he said. More acceleration after the thirteenth step. Marion was gratified that although Montalvo was the crowd favorite, the fans were cheering for her, too. Time for her fourth jump. Time to let it rip.

It was the best jump of the night by any of the competitors, no question about it. But there was no question that it was foul, either. Up in the stands, C.J. held his hands a few inches apart, but the excitement in his face, and Trevor's, sent her another message, too. You were there, they were telling her. You can win this. Go get it. Marion's fifth jump was 22-5, her best effort so far, but she was still in third place behind May and Montalvo. One last chance to win her most difficult event. One last chance to keep the dream of four gold medals alive.

She stood up straight, facing the pit, her face placid. Like the start of a sprint, Marion had a ritual for starting a jump. The crowd clapped in unison, slowly at first but picking up speed as Marion went through her preparations. She bent down, swinging her arms together from her shoulders once, twice, three times, all the while pawing the runway with her left leg as if she were facing a matador. *Clap, clap, clapclapclap.* On the fourth swing of her arms, she raised up, rocked back on her heels, took a deep breath, closed her eyes briefly, and shot down the runway.

Nothing to lose now, she thought, as she ran. Hmm, good approach . . . good takeoff . . . good feeling in the air . . . hey, good jump . . . maybe twenty-three feet . . . maybe good enough to win . . . maybe . . .

Marion was on her knees in the pit, not the most elegant landing in the world, when she looked back and saw the red flag. Damn! A split second passed, she shook her head, then came out of the pit, waving her arms to the crowd that was cheering her effort. She walked over to the official holding the flags, gestured to the takeoff board, shook her head, and grinned at him as if to say, "Ahh, you could have given me that one."

But the official pointed to a strip of plasticine on the foul board, and there—a centimeter over the edge? a millimeter?— was the imprint of her front spike. The call had been good. She had fouled. She had been beaten fair and square.

Moments later, the event concluded with a thrilling last-jump victory of 23-2½ by Montalvo that brought the Spanish fans out of their seats shouting with joy—and provoked the most heated controversy of the World Championships. The television replay on the big screens zoomed in on Montalvo's takeoff and showed that her front foot had gone over the starting board. It had come down, in fact, almost exactly where Marion's foot had been a few moments earlier.

The Italians protested, and May, who thought she had been cheated of victory in the 1995 World Championships, spoke bitterly of quitting the sport. But in the end it appeared justice had been done. Montalvo's foot might have been fractionally over the board, but there was no spike imprint. No mark, no foul. The rules are clear.

"It looked like our feet were in the same place," Marion said, "but how can I complain? It was like a home game in Chapel Hill. If I have four fouls in a game and I foul somebody, they're not going to call it on me."

Carrying her small bouquet of flowers for winning the bronze, Marion embraced Montalvo and Dawn Burrell, who had beaten her in Eugene but had finished sixth here. Then she worked the crowd, who had been begging for autographs throughout the competition, signing pieces of paper and T-shirts and posing for pictures.

At length she moved off to a bench on the infield, sat facing the track, and contemplated the end of the quest for four World Championship gold medals. Her immediate feelings, she realized, were not emotional but practical. The long jump is going to be the hard part in Sydney, too, she thought. The talent is definitely there, but the technique needs work. So fine, she would work on her technique.

"I congratulate Montalvo," she told the press a few moments later. "That last jump showed her character. She earned her victory."

And for herself? Had she tried to do too much? Had she put too much pressure on herself? She didn't regret it at all, she said. She would continue training and competing exactly as she had been. "Of course, I'll be the first one to tell you my long jump needs work," she said with a grin. "My specialty is running."

THE 200-METER DASH had always been Marion's favorite event. There is more room for error, for one thing; the longer distance means a bad start isn't as potentially disastrous as in the 100. Also, the event is less technical. Once up out of the drive phase, there's so much ground to cover, so much time spent just running, that it's almost like being seven years old in Palmdale again.

The fact that the starting blocks are staggered, that nobody is standing next to her, that she can *see* herself beating the competition during the race, is also exciting. Marion can gauge her position, enjoy the feeling of overcoming the other runners, have a sure sense of where she is and how much she is likely to win by. What a wonderful feeling to come off the curve, hug the inside line to keep the distance down to a minimum, pass the last competitor, and race for home.

But perhaps the ultimate reason for Marion's feelings about the 200 were how dominant she had become running it.

She arrived in Seville unbeaten in twenty-two races at the distance since her return to the track, and without a serious competitor in sight. And because the 200 was a 1999 Golden League event, she had competed in it extensively during the summer, generally winning by wide margins. With the 100 and long jump now out of the way, and with competition in the 200 taking place over a leisurely four-day span, her second gold medal seemed to be a lock.

Marion breezed through her first heat Tuesday morning. Though drug testing and her press conference after the long jump had kept her from getting to sleep until after 2 A.M., she was bright-eyed and uncharacteristically chatty on the practice track before the race. No need for a game face this early in the game. And when she eased up toward the end of the heat, virtually jogging the last 10 yards yet still winning in 22.69, the form was set. One more easy heat in the evening, the semifinals on Wednesday, and then a blessed day off before Friday's final. No, she didn't have a worry in the world.

"YOU KNOW SOMETHING," Marion said as she got out of the van back at the hotel where she would relax for several hours. "My back feels a little tight. It's nothing major, but I feel it."

This was no surprise. In seventy-two hours, she had run four rounds of the 100, long jumped eight times, and run a heat in the 200. The Seville track was hard and lacked the underlayer of padding common to U.S. tracks, which was one reason the times were so fast. So why wouldn't her back be sore? Surely it was nothing to worry about. Her back hadn't bothered her since early March when she had felt some stiffness. Steve Bernabeu had come down from Virginia to work out the kinks and after a few days off she had been fine.

Driving back to the track several hours later, the tightness was still there. Steve, and Marvin Finger, Marion's massage therapist, tried to ease the pain on tables they had set up near the practice track in a common area crowded with dozens of athletes. Maybe she was dehydrated, somebody suggested, and she gulped water before going out on the track to loosen up in the blazing late-afternoon heat. Whatever it was, she felt tight as she loosened up with Chandra Sturrup. She could particularly feel it during her quick-movement drills—leg lifts, skipping, jumping. Her mobility was definitely restricted.

Let's get off this hard track and warm up on the grass, Trevor said. All we have to do is get through this evening because there's only one round tomorrow and then a day off. Let's just get through tonight.

Her back felt tight as she went through the pre-race rituals, bending over, stretching, pounding her legs. Aches and pains come with the athlete's territory, though, and Marion put it out of her mind.

Hey, not bad, Marion thought after winning her heat in 22.45, easing up again at the end. She could have picked it up if she'd had to. To run 22.45 in this heat said a lot about the kind of shape she was in. Maybe the stiffness was nothing. Some rest tonight and she'd be ready.

Forty-five minutes later, after cooling down and chatting with the press in the mixed zone, she was no longer so confident. As she put on her clothes, Marion could feel her back with every movement. It's getting worse, she told C.J. Back in her hotel room, a nervous medical crew—Steve, Norm, Marvin—examined, massaged, and tried to give her some relief. Another night without much sleep lay ahead.

THE NEXT MORNING Marion's medical team went to work trying to relieve the pain in her back, which had worsened overnight. Steve Bernabeu tried to manipulate an acupuncture needle into her lower back, but her muscles were far too tight.

"I think I'm starting to feel spasms back there, too," she said. "If I could only pinpoint the area."

If she bent to the left, Marion discovered, the pain was on her left side. Bend to the right and it traveled with her. At least she had the whole day to relax and let Steve and Marvin do what they could for her. The 200 semifinals didn't begin until 7:30 P.M.

An additional concern was the fact that Trevor was busy with other runners. Antonio Pettigrew and Jerome Young had qualified for the final of the 400 meters, and he was off supervising their workouts. By the time he returned to the hotel, there was no real opportunity to get a full update or to consider the drastic idea of not running. Not knowing in detail how much treatment Marion had received, and how ineffective it had been, the coach's mindset remained the same as the athlete's: Gut it out through one more race and then rest for forty-eight hours before the final.

On the practice field, Marion felt as if everyone was watching her. Constant massage and treatment in the cramped training area might send out rumors of trouble, so the entire crew moved off into the grass infield where Steve and Marvin massaged, manipulated, and stretched until it was time to go.

Inside the stadium, there was one blessing at least. For the first time since she had arrived in Seville, it was actually cool. There was even some cloud cover, a summer rarity in this part of Spain, and a full moon. It was a night made for a promenade, or a 200-meter semifinal. All she had to do was run the distance and finish among the first four. Then she could rest for two days.

Inger Miller, letting up near the finish line, won the first semifinal in 22.17. Fast, very fast. The final on Friday was going to be a great race.

Marion's name was called and her face appeared on the big stadium screen. Standing in front of the blocks in lane three, she waved her arms in acknowledgment, but there was no smile. She looked stressed, she thought, when she saw the replay later, not unflappable, as she had at the start of the 100. She frowned a little, approached the blocks quickly, got into the crouch, and listened for the gun. When she looked ahead of her one last time before lowering her head, her face was blank. A silence descended over the stadium.

It wasn't her best start, but that didn't bother her. It was the 200, her race. There was plenty of time to make up ground, plenty of time to be there at the end. And, besides, she didn't even have to win.

She felt fine into the curve, moved up, challenged for the lead. Now there was centrifugal force to contend with, a force powerful enough to break a shoe. Just get through the curve, just get out onto the straightaway, just get pointed toward the finish line, just get . . .

. . . *Damn!* . . .

Marion could feel it the moment she came off the curve, her back tightening and beginning to spasm worse than ever. For a split second she tried to fight it and continue running. She tried to pick up her knees to start her move, but her back wouldn't allow it. She had lost control over her body. Talent, technique, training, will—none of it could help her. She *always* had control over her body, and now she didn't.

"I knew that if I couldn't get my knees up, and if the spasming didn't stop, I was going to stop running, or I was going to take it to the ground," she said later. "I was so scared."

She took it to the ground, her left leg splaying out to the side at an ugly, awkward, dangerous angle. She reached back with her left hand to grab her back, pitched to the right, cushioned the fall with her right hand, and rolled into lane two where she lay on her back, her knees in the air, her face a contorted mask.

Just let me lay here a minute, she thought. Maybe the pain will go away. The noise level in the stands fell to a hush as all the air seemed to have been sucked out of the stadium.

Standing at his seat, C.J. pounded the air with his fist, while in a different section, Marion Toler cringed and wondered if there could be any more suffocating feeling for a mother than this. Trevor, feeling a runner's kinship, seemed to sense a part of himself separating from reality, lying down on the track with Marion. It wasn't a disk injury; he could tell that much by the way her back had seemed to reach up and grab her. He had once had a back injury himself, so he knew. It was a muscle, not a disk. He was sure.

Cameramen approached, and the entire stadium was given a close-up view on the large screens of Marion lying on the track. Two men with a stretcher followed, then C.J. Now it was her right hand clutching her back, and her head was thrust rigidly to the sky as she was lifted onto the stretcher and carried through the tunnel into a medical room off a main corridor.

For a brief time, there was chaos in the small room that could only accommodate eight or ten people, plus a few young volunteers watching the meet on television in the back. Crying with pain and frustration, her back still spasming, Marion rebuffed the U.S. team doctors who wanted to examine her. Norm and Steve, the doctors who knew her best, would be there soon.

The presence of Trevor and C.J., weeping themselves, offered some reassurance, as did the arrival a little later of her mother. Be calm, Marion Toler told herself. Don't be emotional. You must go to a different place now. Then she whispered in Marion's ear: "Everything is going to be all right. Just think about getting well. Nothing else. You're my baby. You're special."

Norm tried to figure out a way to give Marion injections without making her shift from the comfortable position she had found. Finally a nurse just cut off her track pants with a pair of scissors and he gave her a shot of Toradol to ease the pain and Valium to control the spasms. The Toradol burned terribly and Marion's screams filled the room.

The spasms made it difficult for Steve or Norm to make a completely confident diagnosis, but there was some perverse reassurance in that. The spasms had been more than enough to knock Marion off her feet, and there was no reason to think there had been any disk or spinal damage. And indeed, as she lay quietly, the spasms began to moderate.

There's no way she's leaving here on a stretcher, Steve told himself, and he carefully worked on Marion's lower back then wrapped it tightly. Finally, after about an hour and fifteen minutes, she sat up and asked C.J. to help her take her first steps, to the bathroom.

An hour later the fastest woman in the world covered 100 meters down an indoor practice track to a waiting van in a leisurely two and one-half minutes. Every step delivered an electric shock to her back, but just the sight of her walking lifted Trevor's spirits. "That made me feel real good," he said.

From its nearby post in the mixed zone, the media found its view of Marion's departure blocked, but Spanish television cameras were waiting outside the tunnel as the van emerged. Marion's face suddenly appeared on the stadium screens followed by a tape that had already been shown over and over again. She was running, she was falling, she was lying on the track.

At the hotel Marion's tears came and went as did those of the others in the room: C.J., Trevor, his wife, Ann. Finally they left her in the darkness, a pillow propped under her knees, where she turned one way, then another, unable to get comfortable. Yet another night of little sleep had begun.

Back at the track, the reaction to Marion's injury was swift and profound.

"I was watching the TV and saying, 'Where is she?'" said Inger Miller, whose excellent time in the first semifinal promised such a scintillating final. "I know how she runs. She's usually in front."

Australian sprinter Nova Peris-Kneebone said it was tragic and called Marion the wonder woman of track and field. "I would have loved to see her win the gold in the 200," she said. "It would have been an incredible achievement."

"We're athletes," said Michael Johnson, who would set a world record at 400 meters a day later. "We get injured, especially when you're out there running as fast as Marion does. I don't think we need to second-guess her. You're hungry and you're out there to win. I applaud her for it."

Even Primo Nebiolo was moved to make a statement. "I was deeply affected by the injury sustained by Marion Jones," the

IAAF president said, "and I am sure that millions of fans around the world share this sentiment. Marion Jones has become a symbol of all that is best in athletics—enthusiasm and the simple joy of competing."

THERE ARE TIMES, Marvin Finger believes, when a massage therapist can feel not just physical distress but emotional anguish as well. The next morning was one of those times. Working on the upper left quadrant of Marion's back, Marvin could feel the sorrow as clearly as if it were a torn muscle.

"You're really sad, aren't you?" he said. Marion nodded her assent.

The grin on Norm Levin's face told a different story. There was no disk damage. He was sure now. The spasms were subsiding. The pain was abating. There were no symptoms of pain radiating from any one area, and no numbness. Marion was shifting positions and walking more easily with each passing hour.

The big concern now was not physical—compared with the severity of some of her past injuries, this one barely registered—but emotional. Marion's habit of crawling into a shell after being hurt, of becoming sullen and withdrawn for long periods as she had when she broke her wrist in high school and her foot in college, was what needed to be monitored now. The immediate prognosis was not good.

Waking up to the reality of the end of her season, the end of a year's work, Marion was miserable. She turned away sympathetic phone calls and visits from anxious friends and teammates. She refused Steve's suggestion to go outside for a short walk. When her room service order wasn't quite right, she fumed. When C.J. tried to help, she wanted him to just leave her alone. The last thing she wanted was people trying to monitor the condition of her body or her mind, trying to tell her how sorry they were. The last thing she wanted was to be around people at all.

"Poor C.J., he got the brunt of it all," she said. "He went across the street to a candy store where they had my favorite kind of sour licorice. And he got ice cream, too. He was so sweet and patient."

Later in the day they watched a few movies they had brought from home and Marion went to bed early. Her back made it impossible to get comfortable, and the crying jags overwhelmed her once again.

THE NEXT DAY, the mourning was over. Marvin could sense her friskiness during her morning massage. Steve, seeing the change in mood, again suggested a walk. Marion, smiling for the first time since her fall, agreed. She was tired of seeing this room, she thought. Let's get out of here.

She became a tourist. Marion and her mother visited Seville's famous cathedral, its Tower of Gold, its bullfight ring and museum. They rode down the Guadalquivir on a ferry, shopped, took pictures, had lunch. Her hat and sunglasses were an insufficient shield from the public—"Are you okay, Marion?" "Will you sign this, Marion?" "Can we take our picture with you, Marion?" —but still it was a lovely day.

The back spasms were gone now, and while the tightness remained, her mood was light. Physically she would need time to recover, but emotionally she had already seen it through. For the first time in her life, she had suffered the blow, felt the frustration and disappointment for a day, and then moved on. It may have been, she thought later, one of her most important victories.

Running in the 200-meter final that night, Inger Miller set her fourth personal best of the meet and won the world championship she so richly deserved. Her time, 21.77, was .04 faster than Marion's best of 1999.

"Of course, I wanted her to be in the race," Inger said when asked about Marion's absence. "I feel bad for her because I know how it feels. But we've got plenty of time to race, and after she rehabs, I'm sure she'll come back strong and we'll have a good rivalry going next year."

Marion wouldn't speculate about what might have happened. She understood Inger's desire to race and beat the best, and she was impressed by her fast time. Still, she wasn't ready to concede.

"I've always enjoyed pressure situations," Marion said of what might have been a race for the ages. "It would have been interesting to see."

## 10

*N*othing had changed, and everything had changed.

She was still going for five Olympic gold medals, Marion insisted shortly after arriving back home. Nothing that happened in Seville changed that. Her belief that she could still win five remained unshakable, but she would go about it differently.

They had to stop looking at Marion as some sort of superwoman, Trevor believed. They had to understand that her mental toughness sometimes masked indications that something was physically wrong. "We've got to remember she really is human," he said.

So there would be fewer meets in the summer of 2000, and far fewer meets in Europe. Less traveling, no chasing after the Golden League grail, fewer photo shoots, fewer trips for press conferences promoting meets weeks in advance. There would be only one goal now, the Olympics.

There were so many doubters now, Marion knew, so many

people saying she had attempted too much, put too much pressure on her body. If she couldn't win four golds in Seville, they were saying, how could she even think of trying for five in Sydney? Months after the World Championships, Inger Miller declared that she would have won the 200 in Seville whether or not Marion was in the race, and that she would be happy to spoil Marion's plans for the Olympics. "It's not just going to be the Marion Jones Show," she told a reporter.

She would feed on those doubts, Marion told herself. She would think about them on winter mornings at Paul Derr Field when she was wondering why she was out there freezing and working so hard. "This is just going to make everything so much more exciting," Marion said. The fact that the competition was getting better, that so many women were running so fast and setting their sights on the Olympics, would motivate her even more.

Her back would require careful watching, of course. An MRI and numerous X rays revealed a previously undetected genetic condition that caused a strain on the left spinal erector. Dr. Taft prescribed a regimen of ultrasound and exercises to strengthen Marion's abdominals, lower back, glutes, and hamstrings.

Late in October Marion returned to the track for the first time since Seville. Just some light jogging, nothing strenuous, and always she was careful to stop when her back began to tighten up. Then, one day in November, she realized the pain was gone. She could work as hard as she chose, perform the most punishing drills, run as fast as she wanted to, and there was no pain. She was 100 percent now. It felt wonderful.

In the days after she returned home, Marion logged on to the Internet, checked out the chat groups, and began counting the reasons being given for her fall: the hard track, the long jump, the heat, the heats. Too many meets. Too much traveling. She bought the hard-track theory and she couldn't dismiss the idea that the long jump may have jammed her back a bit. But in the end she came to believe that the truth is probably simpler. "Maybe it was just a way of my body saying, 'You've pushed me long enough, and it's time for you to rest,'" she said. "It just happened at the worst possible time."

Finally, as she knew it would, everything came back to the long jump. What had once been a steady drip of common wisdom—she should give the event up, she needed a different coach—became a flood after Seville. And the more Marion heard it, the angrier she became. The hell with those people, she thought. Where were they when she was heavy and slow and coming back from basketball? Trevor was the one who showed her the way, who taught her what she needed to know, who told her over and over that she could do it. She wouldn't trade him for the world.

Nor would she consider, even for a minute, giving up the long jump. She planned to jump every chance she got in 2000—in practice and in meets. She would jump *more* than she had the year before. This time she would be ready.

WHILE AWAY FROM the track, Marion had time to enjoy with C.J. the construction of a new home in Chapel Hill, to celebrate their first anniversary with a vacation, and to indulge in a dream she has had many times.

In her dream, she wakes up from the sleep of the dead. It is eighty or eighty-five degrees. Her room-service eggs are perfect. Her orange juice is freshly squeezed. There is a bagel *and* an English muffin *and* toast on her tray. Her ride to the track is on time and the driver is cordial. There is no crowd holding her up at the gate, no officials suspiciously eyeing her pass. Even the birds are chirping in a certain way.

She is pleased with her warm-up and Trevor gives her his little nod that says he thinks it went well, too. C.J. gives her a kiss and she walks over to the track. There is a slight breeze, just under the allowable limit. As she lowers herself into the starting blocks, she remembers all those days when she threw up after practice and couldn't feel her legs. She is consciously thinking of what she has to do: drive phase, transition, head down, cycling motion, don't lean at the tape.

Her reaction to the gun is perfect, her hands come up high, her stride is fluid every step of the way. Midway through the race, she is well ahead of the other runners and she hears their breathing and their feet behind her.

But she does not feel she is running particularly fast. She thinks it is just an ordinary race, nothing special, and this seems odd because she is so far ahead. Then, when she crosses the finish line, she looks at the clock and sees she has done something nobody has ever done before.

She has run a perfect race. She has set a world record. She has been flying like the wind.

# Part 3

# *The Olympics*

*I*n February 1998 Marion ran two races in Australia, a country whose people, beaches, and weather she had fallen in love with on a previous trip. While in Sydney, she was invited to accompany Michael Johnson and Australian quarter-miler Cathy Freeman to the Olympic Stadium, which was then under construction. How magnificent this is, she thought, as she stood in the uncompleted stands, which were strewn with nails, seeing the enormity of a structure that, in the fall of 2000, would hold 110,000 people. It looked like a city within a city.

The track was not in place yet, but her guides pointed out where the dashes would start, the finish line, and the location of the long-jump pit. Looking around, she tried to picture where the victory podium would be and where C.J. might be sitting, and Trevor and her mother and her brother.

She saw herself taking a victory lap around the track and then standing on the top step of the podium, waving to the crowd, crying unashamedly, a gold medal hanging from a ribbon around her neck.

Some months later, Marion saw pictures of the completed stadium. It was, she thought, even more beautiful than she had imagined.

## 11

*M*arion began her Olympic season as a spectator. Late in March of 2000, C.J. and several of her teammates competed in a low-pressure meet in Raleigh, and as Marion watched she remembered the 1996 Olympics when she had sat seething on the sidelines. But as much as she wanted to run, she knew it was best to wait.

There was no question about her physical condition now—her back hadn't bothered her for months—but she and Trevor had agreed upon a plan and she had to stick with it. She would open her season April 16 at a meet she had loved since high school, the Mount San Antonio College Relays, running a race she hated, the 400 meters.

"I've never trained for the 400 like I did this year," Marion said as she sat at the side of the track at Paul Derr Field. "The workouts weren't always a lot of fun, but I knew I was ready to run. I was just so anxious to get started. For two weeks before the meet, I had trouble sleeping."

Marion had no sooner arrived at Mount Sac than she found a

surprise waiting for her. Though Inger Miller hadn't run the 400 in years, she was entered in the event, too. In fact, Inger said, reprising her statement of the previous summer that the Olympics weren't going to be "just the Marion Jones show," she was thinking of trying for four gold medals in Sydney: the 100 meters, the 200, and the 4×100 and 4×400 relays. She would leave the long jump to Marion.

Marion was both amused and delighted by the news. It all seemed to be in keeping with the reputation Inger's management group, HSInternational, was developing for the flamboyant way its athletes—including the effervescent Maurice Greene, the world record holder at 100 meters—liked to promote themselves.

But whatever Inger's motivation, her presence in the race added to a fine field, which included two international runners, Donna Fraser of Britain and Fatima Yusef of Nigeria, as well as Latasha Colander-Richardson and Monique Hennagan, two fast-developing Americans. Unlike the previous year, when so many 400-meter runners had refused to run against Marion at Mount Sac, this was going to be a real test.

The moment she stepped out onto the warm-up track, Marion created a buzz. As her fellow athletes watched her warm up and run some short sprints, they could quickly see what she had known for months: She was completely healthy.

"Marion scares me and she doesn't even run my event," teased Ato Bolden, the gregarious sprinter from Trinidad who won the world 200-meter championship in 1997. "If I had to run a 100 today and Marion was in the lane next to me, I'd be scared."

STARTING THE RACE FROM THE MIDDLE of the track, Marion at first stayed close to her Paul Derr Field teammates, Latasha Colander-Richardson and Julian Reynolds. Then, coming out of the first turn, she took the lead and began pulling away. The strategy was not surprising because this was her sole open 400 of the year, the race that would establish her credentials for the Olympic 4×400 relay team. So there was only one goal: run as fast as she could for as long as she could.

By the time Marion hit the backstretch, it was clear the race was hers, but more important to her was how she felt. She felt wonderful. "There was a little bit of wind and that was good," she said later, "and when Trevor called out my split at 200 meters—23.02—I knew I was exactly where I wanted to be. I just took off."

Increasing her lead with every stride, Marion ran until she had nothing more to give. About fifty meters from the finish line, she gave out and remembered why she disliked running the 400: her inability to keep her legs pumping high, her lack of arm movement, the burning feeling in her chest.

But even this was a good sign. The last three times she had run the 400, she had felt winded and unable to control her body far sooner, usually with about 100 meters to go. To have felt so strong for so long showed what kind of shape she was in, even if her late fade confirmed what she always told those who said that if she concentrated on the 400 she could set a world record: "I'm not a quarter-miler."

Marion was still well short of the finish line when the crowd rose to its feet and began to cheer. Despite her problems in the homestretch and despite the excellent field, she was winning the race by a huge margin. Nobody needed a clock to tell them what was happening. Marion Jones was back.

Marion's time, 49.59, was the fourth fastest ever run by an

American woman, and fast enough to have won the World Championship at Seville the previous summer. She was so dominant, in fact, that Latasha, who was second, was more than a full second behind her at 51.16. Inger finished more than five seconds later and was last. She blamed her poor performance on having spent time earlier in the week running for a photographer from *Sports Illustrated.* She didn't run another 400 the rest of the year, and never spoke of winning four Olympic gold medals again.

Had she sent a message to Inger? Marion was asked in a crowded press tent later.

"I was sending a message to my brain," Marion said. "It said, 'I'm back and I'm ready to run fast.' There was some emotional buildup because of what happened in Seville. But I've taken care of it. I've moved on."

Over in Australia, Cathy Freeman, the 400-meter world champion and the favorite to win the event in Sydney, quickly learned that Marion had run a faster time than she had posted in almost three years.

"Her reaction was annoyance, anger, and to train harder," Freeman's coach, Peter Fortune, told the *Sydney Morning Herald.* "She was impressed, too. She wanted to do better, so it had a positive effect."

As to whether Marion had proved she belonged on both Olympic relay teams, Don Bosley of the *Sacramento Bee* wrote, "Yes, all right already, we'll let Marion Jones run the 4×400 at Sydney. We'll let her run the entire four laps by herself, if she wants. We'll let her pole vault or sell concessions or mow the infield grass while she's playing the banjo. Anything, anything she feels like, because after Sunday there are no more arguments."

TWO WEEKS LATER, MARION went to another of her favorite stops on the U.S. track circuit, the Penn Relays, to run her final relay legs of the year before the Olympics. A venerable three-ring circus of a meet now in its second century of competition, the Penn Relays drew thousands of high-school and college athletes from around the country and some Caribbean nations, as well as a smattering of America's greatest track stars.

During the three days of competition, a festive atmosphere spilled out of Franklin Field, the old brick stadium on the University of Pennsylvania campus, into the streets of the Philadelphia neighborhood around it. Vendors set up booths along the pedestrian-jammed sidewalks and sold everything from T-shirts, caps, posters, and CDs to sausages, cheesesteaks, and, from several Jamaican entrepreneurs, plates of curried goat.

Celebrities like Bill Cosby and George Steinbrenner patrolled the stadium infield while dozens of races were run one after another at a dizzying pace and tens of thousands of knowledgeable fans—almost 50,000 on the final day—gave a glimpse of how, properly promoted and nurtured, track and field can take hold in a community. From his station in the infield, USA Track & Field CEO Craig Masback, who was promoting a new "USA vs. the World" relay competition, was all smiles.

Marion was scheduled to run in two relays, the 4×100, which the U.S. women would be favored to win at the Olympics, and the 4×200, a distance that is seldom run in world-class competition. These would be her first races of the season at her favorite distances, and she was swept up in the anticipation, the chance to work with her future Olympic teammates, and the excitement generated by the thousands of high-school and college athletes.

On April 28, the day before they were to compete, the U.S. relay teams gathered at nearby St. Joseph's College to practice hand-offs when a problem arose. The women running the 4×100 were set—Chryste Gaines, Torri Edwards, Inger Miller, and Marion running anchor—but there was a dispute over the 4×200. As the defending world champion at 200 meters, Inger insisted on running the anchor leg. But John Capriotti of Nike, who was in charge of putting the team together, thought the honor belonged to Marion because of her domination of the event the previous three years.

"Egos," Capriotti muttered with a pained expression on his face after Inger said if she didn't run the final leg, she wouldn't run at all.

Capriotti came up with a new plan. Since there were plenty of good runners on hand, why not have *two* U.S. teams and let Marion and Inger both run anchor? Depending on how close the race was after three legs, in fact, they could run against each other in an approximation of the 200-meter showdown they had been denied at the World Championships in Seville after Marion had been injured. It could be exciting, Capriotti thought.

The following day, the 4×100 was run first, and though the U.S. team's handoffs were not smooth—Marion received the baton from Inger particularly late—its time, 42.33, was a Franklin Field record and the fastest clocking of the year in the world so far.

About an hour later, as the women gathered for the 4×200, Capriotti was scowling at his clipboard once again. Inger, claiming injury, had dropped out of the race.

"If she was ready to run, I'd have put her out there," Inger's coach, John Smith, told reporters at the side of the track.

Was she going to run the anchor? a reporter asked. Smith said no.

Capriotti rolled his eyes in disbelief. "She wanted to run anchor and I said no way," he said, after hastily redrawing the two U.S. teams. "So we called her bluff. She could have run anchor but she didn't want to run against Marion. It was as simple as that."

LaTasha Jenkins, Latasha Colander-Richardson, and Nanceen Perry ran the first three legs, and as Marion stood in the backstretch to receive the baton, Nanceen was well in front. But even though there was no doubt about the outcome of the race, there was an audible gasp from the crowd and then a roar as Marion, running her first competitive 200 since falling to the track in Seville, came around the curve and headed down the straightaway.

"I knew there probably wouldn't be anyone in front of me," Marion said later, "but it was wonderful coming off that turn. It's so exciting when you hear the people in the stands oohing and aahing. You just want to bring it on home."

The noise grew louder and chants of "USA! USA!" broke out as Marion increased her lead with every long stride and left the other runners almost comically far behind.

"This is like Secretariat at the Belmont!" a television announcer shouted as Marion, crossing the finish line five seconds ahead of the second U.S. team, raised her arms, waved to the crowd, and grinned.

For a moment, there was some confusion as the public-address announcer noted that the time, 1:27.46, was a new American record. No, *wait*, the voice boomed out. It's a *world* record, breaking the mark set by an East German team twenty years ago. And while no one could be certain, Marion's relay leg, 20.8 unofficially, may well have been the fastest ever run.

Marion celebrated with her teammates, clapping the baton into her free hand to applaud them as she walked back to the finish line.

"It's her attitude," Nanceen Perry said as she spoke of being a part of Marion's first world record. "She doesn't have a lot of ego. Her heart is what sets her apart for me."

"To be a part of a world record with this group of young ladies is definitely going to be a highlight of the season for me," Marion said. "Hopefully one of many."

MARION RAN HER FIRST 100-meter dash of the season in Osaka, Japan, on May 13. Her time, 10.84, was the best in the world so far and well ahead of Chandra Sturrup's second-place clocking of 11.07. The fact that she felt a little shaky technically was almost reassuring in a way, she thought. Once she brushed up on her technique, she would be running 10.70 or better, a time no other world-class runner currently seemed capable of approaching.

But the meet also marked her debut in the long jump and the results were not as heartening: a jump of 20-7, her worst performance since returning to the track in 1997, and a fifth-place finish. Within days, rumors began appearing on the Internet that with the Olympics fast approaching she would have to bow to the inevitable, give up the long jump, and compete in four events in Sydney, not five.

Marion just laughed. As a matter of fact, she had *added* the long jump to her schedule for an upcoming meet in Raleigh to get more work in. But Osaka did make one thing clear: She would have to make some changes.

Since the end of the 1999 season, Marion and Trevor had become used to the criticism that they should bring in another coach to help with the long jump. Mike Powell, the retired world record holder, was telling anyone who asked that he was just a phone call away. But Marion and Trevor were convinced they could do the job themselves, and as the season began, they went to work.

Marion's takeoff was restructured—head up, chest out. Her last four steps before hitting the board were altered to give her more height. They worked on staying more relaxed in the air and getting more leg extension on her landing. Marion and Trevor also broke her jump down on video, dissected every motion step-by-step, tore apart each aspect of her technique, and then put it all back together again. She felt much more confident, she said early in the spring. She was excited about how it was coming together.

But Osaka changed everything. Not only had Marion jumped poorly, she had felt so uncomfortable doing it. There simply wasn't time to start over again, she and Trevor realized, not if she was also going to keep training for the sprints. So they decided to go back to the beginning, back to the form that had twice brought her within a quarter inch of a twenty-four-foot jump in 1998. If she was going to win an Olympic gold medal in the long jump, she would do it with her one trait that more technically proficient jumpers lacked: her speed.

"Marion will run right off the board and hang as long as she can and jump far, instead of going scientific," Trevor told a reporter. "I don't care if she lands on top of her head, as long as she wins and stays healthy. When they criticize her technique, all I'm going to say is, 'Did she win?'"

Rather than agonizing over making such an important technical change so late in the day, Marion felt as if a cloud had been lifted. The 100 and 200 were well in hand. Her excellent performance in the 400 at Mount Sac had prompted Karen Dennis, the coach of the U.S. women's Olympic track team, to say of her quest for five gold medals, "She's the perfect candidate to do it. I sure hope she does it on my clock." The long jump was the one variable, the one challenge she needed to maintain her focus in the coming months.

"What I like right now about the long jump is that it's kicking me," Marion said. "It's challenging me. I thrive on being one of the best in the world, and the fact that I'm not right now motivates me every day."

On June 17, at a meet at Paul Derr Field in Raleigh, Marion twice jumped 21-6. She lost the event to Chandra Sturrup and still had a long way to go, but she had improved by almost a foot in just a month.

"I just have to get a little more confident," she said, "and things will fall into place."

THE FIRST MEET of the season that drew a large number of American and international reporters was the Prefontaine Classic in Eugene, Oregon, on June 24. Marion was entered in the 100 and the long jump, but at a large impromptu press conference at Hayward Field the day before the meet, she was amused to find herself answering questions about more than the competition.

To begin with, there was a gray hooded head-to-ankle track suit designed to cut down on wind resistance, which Nike had tested in a wind tunnel. Marion looked like a speed skater about to take the ice when she appeared on the track, but as Nike design engineer Tobie Hatfield explained it, the suit is far more elaborate than anything Bonnie Blair ever wore.

It contains several different fabrics, Hatfield said, each with a different stretch component, a different texture, and, because a sprinter's arms and legs pump back and forth faster than the torso moves forward, even a different thickness to minimize wind resistance. The suit also has thermal qualities to keep the muscles warm.

"I was a bit skeptical at first because I thought it might restrict my movement," Marion said, "but once I saw the results from the wind tunnel, I became convinced it might make a difference."

The second line of inquiry concerned the "Mrs. Jones" television commercials Nike had begun running in which Marion, with only the lower half of her face visible, portrayed a radio deejay based on a character trying to promote peace between warring gangs in the 1979 movie *The Warriors.*

When she was shown the scripts for the commercials, Marion was intrigued by the subject matter—athletes as role models, equal pay for women athletes, "more love" for track-and-field athletes in the United States—and her performances were so deft that some viewers thought Nike had hired a professional actress. Reporters soon picked up on several of the catchphrases in the commercials, and articles about her in the coming months often contained the words "Where's the love?," "The more the better," and "Can you dig it?"

As to whether the commercials would increase her visibility among the public at large, Marion got her answer early in June when she slipped into Chicago's cavernous McCormick Place convention center during the annual Book Expo trade show for book retailers, publishers, and authors. Sitting quietly at a booth signing copies of her newly released biography, she soon found herself inundated by booksellers and others in the industry who recognized her not as one of the world's greatest athletes, but as the star of a television commercial.

"I was so impressed that people realized it was me and kind of agreed with the message," Marion told the reporters in Eugene.

The press conference went on for close to an hour, when a British reporter arrived and asked a more basic question, one Marion could hear in her sleep by now: "Still focused on the five for Sydney?"

"Nooo," Marion said with a weary smile, and she clapped the man on his shoulder. "It's just come out late today. I'm only going to go for three."

Then she, and the rest of the group, burst into laughter.

AFTER HER FIRST attempt at the Prefontaine Classic, Marion left the long-jump pit grinning with satisfaction. Her jump of 22-10½ not only won the event, it was one of the longest in the world all year. Going back to her old jumping style had clearly been the right decision, and with three months to practice before the Olympics she could feel her confidence level rising.

"I'm excited," she said. "I wish the Olympic Trials started to-morrow."

Her performance in the 100 was less reassuring. Marion easily won the race, but her time, a wind-aided 10.93, made her angry. So did her technique. "My start was horrible and my transition was not very good," she said, making it clear she did not blame the body suit for her problems. "I've got to get better."

The fact that she was having trouble with her sprint technique with the Trials less than a month away was disconcerting. It should be automatic by now, she thought. She should be nailing her starts repeatedly and dominating the races from the beginning.

But Trevor was not concerned. She just needed some work in practice, he said, reminding her of the practice time they had lost early in the year when a sudden cold snap interrupted their routine by driving them out of Raleigh to a track in Miami. All she needed was some sustained training before the Olympic Trials and she'd be fine.

A week later in Rome, Marion competed in her last meet before the Olympic Trials and ran the 100 in 10.91, beating Christine Arron by .08 seconds. Again, the time was not fast enough to suit her, and again, she came off the track muttering about her poor start. The fact that she finished third in the long jump, with a leap of 22-0¼, didn't make her mood any lighter as she went home for one last round of training sessions before the Olympic Trials.

THE TEMPERATURE was in the nineties when the athletes began arriving in Sacramento in mid-July, but no one seemed to mind. California's capital city had gone all out to win the bid to host the U.S. Olympic Trials and was making a huge effort to ensure the meet would be a success.

Hoping to raise its national profile—and still smarting from a recent *Los Angeles Times* article calling it "The Big Easy Chair"—Sacramento had enlisted its top business and political leaders to raise money, sell tickets, and, with a huge commitment of space from the *Sacramento Bee,* to publicize the Trials relentlessly.

Sponsors paid from $50,000 to $200,000 to rent air-conditioned suites at the Cal State Sacramento track that contained theater-style seats, fully stocked refrigerators and bars, and the latest in flat-screen television sets. A large expo area adjacent to the track offered a wide variety of food, demonstrations of cutting-edge computer technology, a booth where spectators could e-mail pictures of themselves home, and even a Christian Science Reading Room.

At each end of the stadium, huge video screens showed excellent pictures of the action, and occasional commercials, which were clearly visible no matter how bright the sun. Squads of Sacramento police provided security, hundreds of young volunteers roamed the grounds, and despite the heat, the 23,000-seat stadium was filled to capacity during the seven days of competition. It was, everyone agreed, a huge step up from the spartan and sparsely attended 1999 National Championships in Eugene, and by the end of the first days of competition there was talk of holding the 2004 Trials in Sacramento, and perhaps some National Championships in non-Olympic years as well.

Marion could feel the excitement the minute she arrived at the airport and saw large signs greeting the athletes. There was definitely a big-meet feeling in the air, she thought, and she remembered how well she had performed under pressure in the past. This was the biggest meet of all so far, she thought, the one that would make or break her Olympic dreams that had begun so long ago. She was pleased to see that she didn't feel nervous, just ready to get started.

Adding to the excitement generated by the venue, the Trials contained several intriguing subplots even before they began.

Michael Johnson and Maurice Greene, the world record holders at 400 and 100 meters respectively, were, after several near misses, finally destined to meet in the middle—at 200 meters.

Inger Miller had given a contentious interview to *Sports Illustrated* in which she said, "I think I'm the best sprinter in the world. I know I'm going to win. The media want to have a story and they've found [Marion]. Well, it will make for an even better story when those five medals don't come to be."

And Jackie Joyner-Kersee, encouraged by her husband and coach, Bobby Kersee, was coming out of retirement to compete in the long jump.

"I thought it was wonderful," Marion said when she heard the news. "It was an opportunity for all of us to see her compete for the last time and selfishly I was excited to get a chance to have her involved in making my first Olympic team. Just having her around was a thrill."

Marion knew what Jackie and Bobby were thinking. The women's long jump was at such a low ebb, particularly in the United States, that if Jackie could get off a decent jump in Sacramento—nothing sensational, just decent—she could make her fifth Olympic team.

"I'm here to find out if a thirty-eight-year-old woman can jump twenty-two feet," Bobby said. "Beating Marion or Dawn Burrell is not what counts. Making the Olympic team is all that counts."

ON FRIDAY, JULY 14, Marion and C.J. began their Olympic Trials competition in fine style. C.J. qualified for the finals of the shot put with one almost-casual-looking toss of 65-8¼, while Marion cruised against a slight headwind in her first heat of the 100 to win in 10.92. Her problems with the start were gone, she noted with satisfaction. Inger won her heat in 11.04.

The long-jump qualifying was not as simple, for Marion or for anyone else. For one thing, the contestants in Marion's flight spent much of their time keeping an eye on the women's hammer throw after several hammers got away and one landed perilously close to an official near the long-jump wind gauge.

"I was concentrating more on the hammer than the long jump," said Marion, who kept her back to the long-jump pit until the last minute before jumping. "At the Prefontaine meet, a man in the stands broke his hand when the men were throwing the hammer, so I was quite aware of what was going on. We all laugh about it, but it's a scary thing."

And then there was the magnetic presence of one of the greatest long jumpers in history.

"We're all competing out there and we all have our own little drills, stretching and things," Marion said. "But every single time Jackie stepped on the runway, no matter what we were doing, we just watched her. I think we all felt that at any moment she could do something amazing and we didn't want to miss it."

By the time the competition was over, only Dawn Burrell had been able to reach the automatic qualifying distance of 21-8, and Marion had to be satisfied with the fifth-best mark among the twelve qualifiers, 21-6¾, while Jackie finished eighth with a mark of 21-0¾ on her last jump.

Sitting next to Jackie in the interview tent afterward, Marion said, "There was no doubt in my mind that Jackie was going to do whatever was necessary to get to the final. She's a competitor, and although she might have struggled with her first two jumps, she has it in her heart and that's all you need."

Jackie and Marion, the old pro in her last Olympic Trials and the young hopeful trying to make her first Olympics, continued bantering with the press for a while until an official called out, "Last question."

"So make it a good one," Marion said to a chorus of laughing reporters as she got up to leave.

Outside the tent, she stopped to sign some autographs when a tall man with a short growth of gray beard and wearing a floppy hat approached and stuck out his hand.

"I'm John Carlos," he said, "and I just wanted to say I'm glad I lived long enough to see you."

"It's an honor to meet you," Marion told the man whose black-gloved salute in 1968 in Mexico City had made him one of the most famous and controversial Olympians of his time.

EARLY SATURDAY AFTERNOON, Marion and C.J. lay side by side on adjacent tables under a blue awning on the practice track next to the stadium. The semifinals of the 100 and the shot put finals would begin at the same time and they both appeared calm and confident as they spoke with their teammates about the enthusiastic crowd that had shown up for the first day of the Trials.

After a time, they got up to go to their separate training areas, and Trevor expressed his pleasure that Marion's start in her heat of the 100 the day before had been so smooth. "I was disappointed with that 10.9 in Rome," he said, "but I'll take the win. Yesterday, she was awesome."

The shot-putters were called to the track, and C.J. left his practice area and strolled out to the practice area where Marion was completing her own warm-ups, and extended a hand. It was one athlete attempting to make the U.S. Olympic team wishing good luck to another, nothing more than that.

Marion got off to another good start and easily won her semi-final in 10.93. Inger won the second heat in 11.10, and as the women returned to the practice track for the hour and a half before they would be called for the final, C.J. took part in one of the great shot-put contests in U.S. track-and-field history.

On his third throw, C.J. improved the personal best he had set in Seville the previous summer and took the lead with a heave of 71-6¾ and raised his arms in triumph. That distance led going into the final round when Andy Bloom went into second place with a personal best of 70-10¾ The spectators near the shot-put area howled, and Bloom and C.J. jubilantly bumped their huge chests together. Bloom, overcome by excitement, then fell to the ground, rolled over in glee, and continued his celebration lying down.

"Let's see if that makes TV," Bloom said with a grin later.

But the best was yet to come, as Adam Nelson put the shot 72-7 on his final throw, the best mark in the world all year and a personal best by more than sixteen inches. C.J. had one last chance, and though his toss of 71-9 was his second personal best of the afternoon—and the fourth of the day by the men who would compose the U.S. Olympic shot-put team—it left him in second place.

"Good things happen to good people," C.J. said later in the press tent of Nelson's winning effort. "It's awesome to see somebody do what they have to do when they have to do it."

Asked if he was disappointed to finish second, C.J. said, "As long as I made the team, that's all that matters to me."

"HUNDRED-METER DASH! WOMEN! FINAL!"

The crowd cheered as the announcement boomed out over the public address system. Marion, who had been sitting on the track behind the start line, gazing off toward the finish, rose to her feet, did some last-minute twisting and stretching, and approached her blocks in Lane 6. She waved as she was introduced, lowered herself to the track, and waited for the gun.

Her start was not the best—what *was* her problem getting going lately anyhow?—but it hardly mattered. Running into a head wind, she quickly accelerated before any of the other runners could establish a lead and began pulling away as she came up out of her drive phase.

She's playing with them, Trevor thought as he watched Marion's exaggerated high-stepping stride during the final twenty meters. Look at her tongue sticking out to the side the way she does in practice sometimes when she's having fun.

Marion crossed the finish line in 10.88, a rapturous smile on her face and her arms open wide above in her trademark V. It took a moment before it hit her, and then there it was. Sixteen years since her dream had been given words, eight years since she had decided not to go to Barcelona, four years since she had broken her foot prior to Atlanta. An Olympian at last.

"Crossing the line, I couldn't have known how emotional it was going to be," Marion said later. "It seems like it just took so long. And to do it in California, in front of so many friends and people who had been following me since I was small, it couldn't have been sweeter."

After the medal ceremony, Marion was delayed going to the interview tent when she stopped to hug and chat with her mother and Albert, her friends Bernadine and Janelle Simon, and a surprise visitor to the Trials, her Thousand Oaks High School basketball coach, Charles Brown. While her seat on the makeshift stage remained empty, the first questions were for Inger, who had finished second in 11.05, and Chryste Gaines, who was third at 11.13.

"What do you mean 'make up the time'?" Inger answered impatiently to someone who noted the difference between her and Marion. "The race is over with. That's one race. Why don't you just wait and see what happens in Sydney?"

What about an article Michael Johnson had written for *USA Today* saying Inger might not even make the team? she was asked.

"Maybe he should untwirl those beads in his hair," Inger said. "They're a bit too tight."

Marion arrived just then and was quickly asked about Inger's stated goal of beating her in the Olympics.

"I think it's wonderful," she replied. "We're all competitors and it wouldn't be nearly as exciting if they came out there expecting second. I expect each of them to think they're going to win."

What about the long jump the next day? someone asked.

"Can't I just enjoy this for a couple of hours?" Marion said, drawing a laugh from the reporters.

Inevitably, the questioning then turned to whether Marion might be putting too much pressure on herself at the Olympics by competing in five events.

"If I had a penny for every time somebody's asked me that, I'd be very, very rich," she said.

"You already are," Inger said to a burst of appreciative laughter.

"Maybe that's the wrong choice of words," Marion said with a smile.

Describing her victory in the 100, Marion, still fretting over her start, mentioned some "kinks." Pressed for details, she laughed and said, "Do you want me to tell that in front of my competitors?"

"Go ahead," Inger said to more laughter.

The display of good humor ended when one reporter asked Inger if their rivalry might somehow hurt their collaboration in the 4×100 relay in Sydney.

"We know we have to come together as a team," Inger said. "I don't think anybody here dislikes each other. Rivalries or not, it's not personal. I respect all my competitors and I respect Marion Jones and what she's done for our sport. I just think if I'm going to have an interview, I don't think all the questions should revolve around Marion Jones."

In the days that followed, some reporters noted that as pointed as Inger's remarks about Marion sometimes were, Marion never responded in kind. If there was any bad blood between the two athletes, it all seemed to be flowing in one direction.

LATER THAT EVENING, Marion returned to the practice track for a rubdown when a tall man approached holding the hand of a nine-year-old girl. Marion was delighted to see them, and after an animated chat, she presented the child with a stuffed bear, symbolic of the upcoming Sydney Olympics, which she had been given for winning the 100-meter dash.

"Thank you," Mary Ruth Joyner said as her father, Al Joyner, beamed. "I hope you break my mommy's records."

• • •

LESS THAN AN HOUR after the start of the long jump Sunday afternoon, Marion was in big trouble. Still on a high from her victory the previous day and troubled by gusts of wind sweeping the runway, she fouled on her first two jumps and had only one remaining before the field was cut from twelve to eight. She didn't need a big jump to stay in the competition—a mere twenty-one feet would do—but she did need a fair one.

Sitting in the stand with C.J., Trevor didn't know what to think. On the practice track in the morning, Marion's long-jump drills had been so impressive that Jackie Joyner-Kersee and Bobby had come over to watch. She's going to jump far today, Trevor thought, and when her first jump was smooth and mechanically sound, his reaction, despite the foul, was "Wow, she's putting it all together." But now, one jump later, here she was not only in danger of failing to make the Olympic long-jump team but also facing the ignominy of not even getting all her jumps.

Marion's first two jumps were easily long enough to qualify had she not fouled, but a miscommunication with the judge sitting at the starting line compounded the problem. After her first miss, Marion thought he had indicated that she was only slightly over the line, whereas she had actually fouled by half a foot.

"No, no, you're fouling by more than that," C.J. yelled from the stands when her foot landed on the board the second time.

"Move back farther," Trevor agreed, and when Marion still seemed unsure, he said, "Just move back a whole foot and you'll be fine."

As she prepared for the third jump, Marion felt surprisingly calm. She really was jumping well, she thought. She didn't even need to come close to the board to get off a fair jump. And then there was the help she was getting from Jackie, who was urging her on.

"You've got it today! That one's out there!" Jackie shouted after Marion's first jump. "No problem, just back off a little bit and get a legal jump and you'll go far," she said after the second foul.

Then, as if to show what she meant, Jackie jumped 21-10¾ on her third attempt and moved into fourth place in the competition.

"Don't let them retire you yet!" Bobby shouted from the stands as the crowd erupted in cheers.

Marion paced the head of the runway, closed her eyes, brushed her windblown hair from her face, and puffed her cheeks. She bent forward from the waist, swung her arms forward and back, straightened up, and raised her left foot out in front of her as she reached her full height. She put her foot down, hopped into the air, and was off.

The tension dissipated the instant she left the ground. It was clear she had plenty of room to spare at the starting board—six inches or more—and her jump was more than far enough to keep her in the competition. Her reaction as she rose from the pit and looked back was a quizzical, stoic look, a shake of her head, and then, finally, a wan smile of relief. Marion's jump, 22-1¾, put her in fourth place and knocked Jackie back to fifth. The two women hugged and prepared for their final three jumps.

Marion's reaction to her new lease on life was both physical and emotional. She could feel the spring in her legs and her mind relax. It's out there, she told herself. Blast off now. Go for it. And on her fourth jump she briefly took the lead with a jump of 22-7. Dawn Burrell quickly overtook her at 22-10, and Jackie, fading now, came up short of 22 feet.

"You've got your position now," Trevor told her as she got ready for her fifth attempt. "Do exactly what you did your first two jumps. You've got a big one coming."

At 2:10 P.M., Marion took one last long running step, caught the board with four or five inches to spare, and became the U.S. women's long-jump champion for the year 2000. Her jump of 23-0½ was the third longest in the world to date, less than three inches off Fiona May's top effort, and put her squarely in the running for the Olympic gold medal.

Marion came up out of the pit, walked back toward the head of the runway, and, when the distance was posted, pumped her arms in the air in response to the shouts of the crowd.

"It was such a relief," she said later. "I was like, 'Yes! Yes! Yes!' which is funny because I've jumped 23-11¾ and now I'm so excited to hit 23 feet. But it was great to do it at the biggest meet of my life."

The competition ended with the crowd on its feet as Jackie ran through the pit on her final attempt and Marion followed. More than a little relieved, Jackie had come to terms with the fact that she was not going to make her fifth Olympic team, while Marion, pumped with adrenaline, simply felt too much emotion to get off another jump.

Walking back past the pit for the last time, Marion clapped her hands and waved them above her head, then sought out Jackie and the two women hugged. Jackie handed Marion a water bottle as they left the infield, prompting Joe Davidson of the *Sacramento Bee* to write, "The gesture might as well have been the passing of the Olympic torch."

And just as Marion had been bowled over by Jackie's unaffected warmth and kindness when they first met in Indianapolis in 1997, she could see those qualities asserting themselves again.

"It wasn't this deep emotional ending like everybody wanted it to be," she said of their final conversations at the long-jump pit. "We were just casually chitchatting. It was as if she was saying, 'All right, let me go on home now.' I think I felt worse about it than she did. I would have loved to have been on the same Olympic team with Jackie."

A few minutes later, Marion sat at the finish line and watched the final of the women's 400 meters. To keep Marion off the U.S. 4×400 relay team, four runners would have to better the blazing time she had posted three months earlier at Mount Sac. None did, as Latasha Colander-Richardson won the race with a time of 49.87, nearly three-tenths of a second slower than Marion's best. Pending only the outcome of the 200 the following weekend, Marion's participation in five events at the Olympics was now assured.

"Case closed," said Olympic women's track coach Karen Dennis. "The other women will have to understand. They can deal with it. Quite frankly, on a peg and a leg, I would probably go with Marion."

IN DEFERENCE TO NBC, which scheduled its broadcast of the Olympic Trials over two weekends, the competition shut down for two days, and with only one event remaining, Marion had five days off in the middle of the competition. She made the most of them.

She attended a Sacramento Monarchs WNBA game, went to the movies, attended the Trials as a spectator, signed copies of her new biography in the expo area, visited the city's first settlement at Sutter's Fort, and, in an auditorium near the track, held what C.J. noted was their first joint press conference. The atmosphere was relaxed and the questions for the most part tended toward the trivial and the personal.

Who takes out the trash at home? (She does.) Were they planning a family? (They already have one: C.J.'s children, who spend a great deal of time with them, and their two dogs, Izzy and Paulie.) Why didn't he kiss her after she won the 100? (He was still cramping up from the shot-put finals.)

Finally, a reporter got around to more substantial matters. About those five gold medals, he said . . .

"I'm so proud of you guys," Marion said with a grin. "It's taken twenty minutes for that to come up."

Which question did she wish would go away, someone asked after the laughter had subsided, the five gold medals or her long-jump technique?

"Can't I have my cake and eat it, too?" she said.


As Marion watched the competition one evening from a front-row seat in Nike's luxury box, a slight, trim woman in a graying pageboy haircut entered accompanied by two teenage girls. As she noticed Marion, the woman's eyes brightened and she said how fascinated her daughters were by her. Would it be possible, she wondered, for them to meet?

Dave Mingey, a Nike public relations man, immediately ushered her forward and then it was Marion's turn to be wide-eyed.

"What a thrill it is to meet you," she told Joan Benoit Samuelson, who in 1984 won the first woman's marathon ever run at the Olympics.

As Marion fussed over the girls, Joan asked a bystander how old she was. Twenty-four, she was told.

"24 . . . 28 . . . 32 . . ." she said, mentally ticking off the years. "You know, she should compete in as many Olympics as she wins medals in Sydney. Or maybe she should finish her career by running the marathon."

SUNDAY, JULY 23, was the final day of the Trials, and easily the hottest. But despite the fact the temperature climbed into the hundreds, the stands were full once again as spectators anticipated watching a number of final events. Among them were Michael Johnson's long-awaited 200-meter showdown with Maurice Greene, and Marion's duel with Inger.

Marion had no sooner arrived at the track than she received some surprising news: She would be running against Inger not once during the afternoon, but twice. Both women had won their first-round heats the day before, but Marion's time, 22.62, was more than half a second better than Inger's, and there were several runners in between. So when the formula for drawing up the semifinals was put into effect, Marion and Inger were both placed in the second heat. And, as if to make the point more emphatic, they were in adjoining lanes.

For Marion, the stakes were immediately raised. Yes, it was hot, and yes, she would have to save something for the final less than two hours later, but try telling that to the competitor in her. As much as Marion prided herself on never responding to Inger's challenging remarks in public, she eagerly awaited the chance to answer her on the track.

"I've never been one to trash-talk and I'm not going to start now," was the most she would say on the subject. "If you're going to talk, come out and be ready to run. That's all I'm asking."

As she tinkered with her blocks and got ready for the semifinal, Marion could sense her excitement begin to build. This is what the final should feel like, she thought as she prepared to meet Inger at 200 meters for the first time since Seville. There had been so much talk since then, so many reminders that Inger was the world champion at 200 meters, so much speculation about whether she would have won even if Marion hadn't been injured. It's time to quiet everything down, Marion thought. It's time to move on.

Taking a huge lead in the opening straightaway, Marion made up the stagger on Inger before the turn, and though she eased up at the end, her time, 22.08, was .32 seconds ahead of Inger's second-place finish and by far the fastest in the world to date.

"Why did you run so fast in this heat?" Trevor scolded her back at the practice track. "You've got another race to run."

Marion knew he was right. She had wanted to prove a point and she had let her emotions get the best of her. But she knew something else, too. She had just proved that nobody was going to beat her in the final.

Nobody did, although Inger stayed closer this time before Marion's finishing kick put the race away. Her time, 21.94, was the first sub-22 clocking of the year, and Inger, who finished second in 22.09, patted her on the back after the race.

"The best word I can use to describe this is I'm glad it's over, even though that's more than one word," Marion joked afterward. "I'm pooped."

And what did Inger think about her quest to beat Marion now?

"It's coming," she said. "The show is in Sydney."

FIFTEEN MINUTES AFTER Marion won her third U.S. Championship, matching her record-equaling performance in New Orleans two years earlier, the Trials ended in disarray as Michael Johnson and Maurice Greene both pulled up lame in the final of the 200. The promise that they would provide one of the Olympics' greatest highlights limped off the track with them and, observers noted, ensured that even more of the attention in Sydney would be focused on Marion.

"Jones's bid for five gold medals now becomes *the* American story leading up to the Games," wrote Barbara Huebner in the *Boston Globe.*

As to Marion's performance in the Trials overall, Lynn Zinser of the Colorado Springs *Gazette* wrote, "In ten days full of trash-talk and mind games, Jones was the picture of calm, the voice of reason, pleasant and polite and dominating to the end. Marion Jones was a triumph."

"Marion Jones got exactly what she wanted these past eight days," said Aileen Voisin in the *Sacramento Bee,* "which was everything."

# 12

---

Sydney was chaos. Crowded, noisy, magnificent chaos. The moment Marion and C.J. got off the plane, a security detail hustled them off to a first-class lounge, fetched their bags, and swiftly moved them down a back stairwell to a van. Nobody even knows we're here, Marion thought as they rode through streets on which every storefront, every billboard, every lamppost, said *Olympics, Olympics, Olympics.* How exciting this is.

Marion and C.J. had spent their first three days in Australia in Melbourne, a city she had enjoyed so much during her visit two years earlier. They had read of confusion, massive delays, and lost baggage at the Sydney airport, and the idea of staying out of the eye of the storm until the final moment appealed to them.

Not that Melbourne was exactly peaceful. The track where she worked out had been the site of the 1956 Olympics and was surrounded by photographers, who, when they were told they were not allowed inside, set up a huge crane across the street and stood on top to get their shots. They want pictures of me *practicing* that badly? Marion thought. Amazing.

Marion was delighted to discover that the first U.S. women's soccer game, against Norway, was being played in Melbourne, and she went to the stadium, met with the players, took pictures, sat in the stands, and cheered. It was all so pleasant she was almost sorry to leave.

For several reasons, Marion and C.J. had decided to stay in an apartment complex about twenty minutes from the Olympic Stadium rather than at the Olympic Village. Since her coach and massage therapist weren't official members of the U.S. delegation, they were not allowed in the Village, so simply getting a massage or meeting with Trevor to plan her days would be a problem.

Then there was the fact that postcompetition drug testing and press conferences often kept her up late, which complicated her eating and sleeping schedule. Living in an apartment where they could fend for themselves allowed C.J. to prepare the food she liked—chicken, fish, pasta—in the morning, and it would be ready when they returned. As much as possible, they would avoid the hothouse atmosphere of the Olympics and try to stick to their regular routine.

MARION FELT SUPREMELY CONFIDENT going into the Games. After the Olympic Trials, she spent the month of August in Europe, where she ran an excellent series of races that emphasized just how far ahead of the rest of the world's sprinters she was.

In Stockholm, helped by a trailing wind that was only slightly over the legal limit, she ran the 100 in 10.68, her best time in two years. In Brussels, she ran 10.83 *against* the wind, a time track statisticians said no other runner had ever equaled in such conditions. And twice in the final run-up to the Games, in London and Berlin, she ran 10.78, lowering her own best-in-the-world mark for the year.

The only close call came August 11 in Zurich, where she almost lost a race to Inger Miller. After her first false start of the season, Marion sat in the blocks for an extra beat and then came out of them sluggishly. Inger got off to a superb start and led by several meters almost before the race began. But Marion kept her composure and, relying on her strength in the middle stages of the race, slowly closed the gap. Just before the tape, she caught Inger and surged ahead to win by .01 seconds, in 10.95.

Inger reacted almost as if she had won.

"I think right now I'm in her head because I can run with her all the way down," she told reporters. "I don't think it makes a difference whether I get her now or in Sydney."

Marion had a different view. If no one could beat her after a start as bad as this one, she thought, what chance would they have in Sydney?

"Inger ran a very good race," she said. "Today was her chance."

Marion also entered the long-jump in Zurich and, with a jump of 22-9, defeated an all-star field that contained Niurka Montalvo, the world champion from Spain, Italy's Fiona May, who had the top jump in the world, and Heike Drechsler, the great German Olympian who was still going strong at the age of thirty-five.

But Marion's last long-jump competition before the Games, in Brussels, was less gratifying. She had trouble getting her steps down, fouled four times, and, with a jump of 21-7½, finished fifth.

"It seems like I can't get two events in one meet right," said

Marion, who had run so brilliantly into the wind less than an hour earlier and who had jumped so well in Zurich two weeks before. By now it was clear that her chances in the long-jump competition depended on who showed up in Sydney: the Marion Jones who had trouble jumping twenty-two feet or the one who could fly twenty-three feet and beyond.

"All it takes is one big jump," Marion said. "That's what I'm hoping for."

C.J. WAS OUT OF THE OLYMPICS. One day he was a threat to win the gold medal, the next he was undergoing knee surgery in North Carolina.

Lifting weights before the August 5 meet in London, he had felt some pain in his left knee, but thinking it was just a recurrence of some tendinitis he had been troubled with in the past, he continued to train and compete. Two weeks later, in Brussels, the pain was so bad he passed on his last two throws. After traveling to Berlin with Marion, he underwent an MRI exam, which revealed the damage: a torn piece of cartilage called the "meniscus" in his left knee.

The day after C.J. returned home, Dr. Tim Taft at the University of North Carolina confirmed the diagnosis and operated immediately. While he held out some hope of a recovery before the Olympics, C.J. finally had to accept the fact that there was not enough time. In 1996, when Marion was injured, she had gone to the Olympics to root for him. This time, he would be the spectator. He had been around long enough to know injuries are a constant threat to any athlete, but as Marion prepared for her big moments, that knowledge didn't make it any easier to take.

"I was pretty upset when I first learned about the injury," C.J.

told reporters. "Then I figured I could spend the next fifty years being upset about it or the next month putting all my energies into getting her ready."

"It's every athlete's worst nightmare," said Marion, who thought she might be as disappointed as he was. "I definitely wanted this to be a family affair."

During the first week of the Olympics, Marion was a reluctant tourist. Since track and field is traditionally contested the second week of the Games, its athletes must train and watch and wait while all around them swimmers, gymnasts, and competitors in dozens of other sports are living out their dreams on a worldwide stage.

How was she supposed to keep working out when the Games had already started? Marion asked herself. What was she supposed to do when every time she looked out the window she could see the Olympic rings, when every time she turned on the television set there was another athlete on the victory stand? When was it going to be *her* turn? Then she laughed and realized she had been waiting sixteen years for this moment. She guessed she could wait one more week.

One problem was that it was hard to do much. Except for a movie or two, going out was difficult because it meant coordinating arrangements with her security detail, a couple of New South Wales policemen who wore black shirts with an insignia that read Athlete Protection Unit.

Marion thought nothing of the fact that after two days in Sydney a third man was added to her entourage. Only after the Olympics was she told she had received a death threat that was quickly traced to a college student in Buffalo, New York. There seemed to be no real danger—what master criminal sends a death threat via e-mail?—but Charlie Wells was taking no chances. So the three policemen, all nice, unobtrusive guys who asked to have their picture taken with Marion as the Games were ending, accompanied her wherever she went.

Marion had been looking forward to the Opening Ceremonies but was surprised to discover they were not at all what she had expected. The large U.S. delegation gathered in front of a row of town houses in the Olympic Village, where athletes from various sports, most of them meeting each other for the first time, all seemed to want to take pictures of each other.

"Marion Jones!" a loud voice boomed out amid all the frenzied confusion. "I've been looking for you. Come take your picture with me!"

Marion laughed and happily posed with Tommy Lasorda, the former Los Angeles Dodgers manager who was coaching the U.S. Olympic baseball team.

The U.S. team was taken to the gymnastics arena, where they sat watching the Opening Ceremonies on television for hours as they waited to march into the stadium. Bored and a little frustrated—"I thought the athletes were going to be a part of the ceremonies and really experience it," she said—Marion decided to have her own celebration.

She took out her video camera and, with Antonio Pettigrew in tow, cruised the arena. She posed with Alonzo Mourning and other members of the NBA Dream Team. She clowned with the women's basketball team, and with Mia Hamm and the women's soccer team. She chatted with Venus and Serena Williams. She met boxers and sailors and as many other American athletes as she could. All of them, it seemed, were as excited to be at the Olympics as she was.

Finally, the U.S. team was called to line up—it was amazing

how many of them there were—and as "The United States of America" boomed out over the public-address system, they walked into a stadium filled with lights and music and the noise of more than 100,000 spectators. This is unreal, Marion thought, and she felt overwhelmed by the enormity of it. When Australia's own Cathy Freeman lit the Olympic torch, and the stadium boiled over into an emotional frenzy, she edged as close to the action as she could and kept her video camera rolling.

AS THE OLYMPICS GOT OFF and running, and as Marion watched and waited, two things happened that surprised her. The first was a statement from Carl Lewis that her quest for five gold medals was a mistake. It was wrong for Marion's "people," the former Olympic sprint and long jump champion said, to "put her in that situation."

Marion, who read Lewis's statement on the Internet, was hurt. She was used to people refusing to understand that she was the one who determined her competitive schedule, although it was interesting, she thought, that no one ever told Lewis *he* was overextending himself when he won four gold medals in Los Angeles in 1984. But to hear one of her earliest heroes, one of the people who drew her into track and field when she was a little girl, criticize her goals was truly disappointing.

"I was the biggest Carl Lewis fan growing up," Marion said. "To have someone you idolized say negative things at a time like this was frustrating. I just decided I was at the biggest arena of them all and I couldn't let his words dampen my spirits. I just tuned him out."

Marion could not ignore the importance of the second surprise, however. Inger Miller was out of the 100.

She had strained a hamstring training at UCLA early in September, Inger said two days before the first heats, and though her condition had improved, she was in no shape to run. She still hoped to compete in the 200 and the 4×100 relay a week later, but clearly her availability for those events was in doubt, too.

Inger was dry-eyed and philosophical as she met the press. She couldn't be upset, she said. She had to go with the flow. It was not the end of the world. She wished Marion all the best and was only sorry she couldn't give her some great competition.

Marion understood. Athletes are injured and their events go on without them. She had had to deal with her own injury on the world stage in Seville and listen to some people in Inger's camp suggest she had succumbed to the pressure of the moment and might have lost the 200 to her anyway. It was funny, she thought, how words can come back to haunt you.

But she would miss Inger in the race. You want to compete against the best, and when Inger is healthy and running her race, she is one of the best. She would let it go at that, Marion thought. She had her own races to run.

ON FRIDAY, SEPTEMBER 22, the first day of track-and-field competition, Marion's security detail drove her to the practice track where she would warm up prior to the first heat of the 100. As they rode past the Olympic Stadium, she couldn't believe her eyes. It was only 9:30 in the morning, but the 110,000-seat stadium was full. From the luxury boxes to the seats in the top row, the Australian fans, who some would later say composed the largest and most enthusiastic audience ever to watch a track meet, were waving and chanting and creating an electric atmosphere that would last for ten days.

Marion was still awestruck when she entered the stadium early that afternoon, but she was the picture of calm confidence as her name was called out prior to the first heat of the 100. Her hair in braids woven becomingly to her head, she smiled and waved both hands in the air as the Australian crowd, which had warmed to her pursuit of five gold medals in recent months, cheered loudly.

Marion's only goal in the first round was to nail her start, get it down absolutely right, and put her problems out of the blocks during the summer behind her. Which she did. Trevor beamed with delight as she shot out to a commanding lead and then, just as they had planned, shut down. She won the heat in a leisurely 11.20 and left the track smiling.

Seven hours later, wearing Nike's futuristic body suit for the first time in Sydney, Marion's attitude was different. Staring straight ahead as she adjusted her blocks for the second round of the 100, she waved when her name was called, but now the smile was gone. Time to get serious.

Again, her start was excellent, but this time she ran through the finish line at something approaching top speed. Her time, 10.83, was faster than anyone else had run all year and only one other qualifier broke 11 seconds, Ekaterini Thanou of Greece at 10.99. On Saturday, Marion would go for her first gold medal. It was there for the taking.

"Close your eyes," C.J. told her that night as she lay in bed, going over the race again and again in her mind.

"They *are* closed," Marion said. "I'm just not sleeping."

Trevor's instructions to Marion before the semifinals of an important track meet are invariably the same: Blast out in front to send a message to her mind and her opponents that she is ready. This time, though, he had a different plan. Nail the start, he said, work the middle portion of the race, and then shut it down. Save the big effort for the final.

The wisdom of this strategy was confirmed early Saturday evening when Merlene Ottey won the first semifinal in a relaxed 11.22. No reason to leave anything out on the track now, Marion thought, and she eased way up before the finish line and won her heat in 11.01.

Back in a warm-up area, Marion could feel her emotions running high during the hour before she returned to the track. How could it be any better than this? she wondered. She was at the Olympics, she was running as well as she ever had in her life, and no one seemed capable of keeping up with her. The weather, which had been quite cool before the Games began, was cooperating, too. It was a nice comfortable spring night, without even much wind to worry about.

Standing in Lane 5 behind the start line, Marion betrayed no tension as the runners' names were called. When a stadium cameraman walked up so close he was almost in her face, she leaned in and blew a kiss. Farther away, a television cameraman focused on her glittery new shoes, made of a clear lightweight plastic, that were Nike's latest design.

Marion stood behind her blocks, bouncing from side to side until the call came. She settled into her starting position, put her hands on the track, nervously twisted her wedding ring, and bent her head down to the track, as if in prayer. Then she lifted up her head, leaned forward expectantly, raised her body into the air, and . . . stood up with the other runners as Debbie Ferguson of the Bahamas signaled to an official that she didn't feel comfortable in her blocks.

Marion took a few steps down the track, clapped her hands,

and walked back. In her crouch again, she looked up, got set, and was off with the gun. Which immediately went off a second time.

Ekaterini Thanou, figuring her only chance to win was to get off to the best start of her life, had broken too soon, and the runners walked down the track, then came to the start line for the third time. She had been through this before, Marion told herself, remembering when Merlene Ottey ran halfway to the finish line after a false start at the 1997 World Championships in Athens. Just refocus, she thought. Take a deep breath. Everything is going to be fine.

Three steps out of the blocks, the race was hers. Only Tayna Lawrence of Jamaica, running across the track in Lane 1, was anywhere close at the start, and before the race reached its halfway point, she was well back, too. The only question now was not whether Marion would win, but by how much.

A photo spread in *Sports Illustrated* tells the story. Across two adjacent pages, four runners, led by Ekaterini Thanou, are bunched tightly together. A third page folds out to the right and there, with a vast expanse of open track separating her from the others, is Marion. Her arms are stretched out behind her, her legs are off the ground, her mouth is wide open. The finish line, which she is about to race across with a hop and a fist thrust joyously into the air, is not yet in sight.

Marion's time, 10.75, was her fastest of the year and .37 seconds better than the 11.12 posted by Ekaterini. ("I knew I couldn't beat her," the Greek runner said later. "I said to myself, 'I'm going to be happy with a silver medal.'") The only greater margin of victory in an Olympic 100-meter final by either a man or woman was posted by Marjorie Jackson of the U.S. in 1952. To put Marion's four-meter victory over Ekaterini into perspective, one observer noted, it was the equivalent of winning a marathon by a mile, or the Indianapolis 500 by eight laps.

Marion had planned her victory celebration well in advance. She would wave, she would smile, she would listen to the cheers, she would soak it all in. She would savor each moment so she could relive them the rest of her life. But she would not cry. No babbling, sobbing athlete standing on the podium for her. She would show them how she kept her cool.

She never had a chance.

"The first emotion that hit me was joy, and then excitement," she said later. "Then I took three more steps and I realized that every time they introduce me from now on, instead of saying 'world champion,' it's going to be 'Olympic gold medalist.' The emotion really started to run through me then, and when I looked over at the stands there were my mom and my brother and my uncle and my cousins all at the perfect spot straight ahead of me."

A phalanx of cameras at the side of the track caught her as she bent deeply from the waist, put her head in her hands, and began to cry. She walked over to the edge of a camera well, reached over to hug her mother, kissed Albert, and, smiling through her tears, held up an American flag and one from Belize to carry around the track on an emotional victory lap that was lustily applauded by the Australian fans.

"Here's my new litmus test for an athlete," wrote Christine Brennan in *USA Today.* "If the Aussies cheer, they've found a keeper. And they loved Jones, applauding her long into night. They enjoyed every minute of her lingering victory lap. They treated her as if she were one of their own, not one of ours. That's the ultimate compliment down here."

A short time later, Marion stood on the top step of the podium, cradling the gold medal hanging from her neck in her hands. For several moments, she stared at it, turned it over, read the inscription, held it close. And as her little-girl smile was beamed around the world, no translation was necessary. So this, she was thinking, is what it looks like.

"I had never seen one and I wanted to get a really good look," Marion said later. "It was so beautiful, and so smooth. No rough spots. It's so much better than the dream. It's so much better to have it actually around your neck."

Marion regained her poker face during the playing of the national anthem, but as she sang "the land of the free" her arms shot up into the air and her smile returned. She bent down to exchange a kiss with Ekaterini Thanou and a handshake with Tayna Lawrence, who won the bronze. Then with a final wave to the crowd she climbed down from the podium.

Sixteen years ago, she had written the words on a blackboard: *I want to be an Olympic champion.* And now she was. It was the greatest moment of her career, and it was only the beginning.

THE PHONE RANG later that night.

Marion has no memory of which news agency the caller was from or what his exact words were. Something about a story in the next day's paper. Something about a positive drug test. Something about C.J.

"Please don't call here," she said, and she hung up the phone. Here we go again, she thought.

How many rumors about drugs had she heard over the years? she wondered. Rumors about foreign athletes. Rumors about American athletes. Rumors about her teammates. Rumors about

C.J. Rumors about herself. It was the price of competing in this most cynical of all sports, she had learned long ago. You just had to tune the rumors out.

The next morning, the hurricane struck. Anonymous sources had told the *Daily Telegraph* in Sydney that C.J. had tested positive for nandrolone at a meet in Oslo in July. The news rocketed through Sydney and around the world. Marion had gone from gold-medal winner to wife of an accused steroid user in less than a single day.

Marion and C.J. cried for hours. Her tears flowed freely as they sometimes had in past crises. It was one of the ways she dealt with pain and frustration and it seemed almost natural somehow, a cleansing that let her work things through and start over. But C.J.'s tears were hard to bear. He was seldom one to show strong emotions, even in private, and to see how badly he was hurting increased her own pain to the breaking point.

It wasn't true, he told her. He would never do a thing like that, not ever, and certainly not now when it could hurt her so badly. Marion looked him in the eyes and knew he was telling the truth. She had no doubts. None. She would stick by him, she told him. Remember all the times he had been there for her? Now it was her turn. She had complete faith in him. It would be difficult, she said, but they would get through it. And then they cried some more.

In the next few hours, as she and C.J. made a few phone calls and tried to decide what to do, Marion could sense her emotions changing. The pain gave way to feelings of despair and helplessness and then, after a time, to a deep, abiding anger.

Who would want to do this? she wondered. Why, in the middle of the competition, would a story appear concerning a two-month-old drug test of an athlete who wasn't even *in* the Olympics? The timing was highly suspicious, not to mention the fact that the story had been leaked by unidentified sources whose information could not be examined or challenged. Somebody, it was clear, had a private agenda, and the more she thought about it the more she came to believe that agenda was not to hurt C.J. It was to hurt her.

During the next few days, the Olympics descended into an unparalleled bout of ugly self-destructive recriminations. Members of the International Olympic Committee hurled charge after charge against the IAAF, the international governing body of track and field, which had administered the test C.J. had allegedly failed, and at the U.S. Olympic Committee and USA Track & Field, which were accused of knowing about the test results and covering them up.

But this has nothing to *do* with the Olympics, IAAF secretary-general Istvan Gyulai told the AFP news agency. "I regret that this news is breaking when Marion Jones is running," he said. "It's terrible whether it's true or not. If it's not true, it would seem there are efforts to smear the wonderful days here."

The IOC was unrepentant. Dick Pound, a vice-president from Canada, was the first to go on the record, saying "a reliable source" had told him C.J. had failed the test although he didn't have "any personal knowledge." (Pound, it was recalled by Canadian reporters with some amusement, had given his country's official defense of Ben Johnson before Johnson was sent home from Seoul in disgrace in 1988 for using steroids.) Jacques Rogge of Belgium, an executive board member and vice-chairman of the IOC medical commission, said C.J. should be stripped of his accreditation and told, "Sir, you have no place in these Games."

Pound and Rogge were among the leading candidates to replace Juan Antonio Samaranch, who was retiring as president of the IOC after the Olympics, and it was clear that they were using the report of the drug test to lobby for the support of their colleagues by pummeling a villain many in the international Olympic community had come to detest: the United States.

Americans had long been accused of hypocrisy where drugs were concerned and many thought they had it coming to them. Some of the same U.S. coaches who complained about foreign swimmers whose times improved dramatically, for instance, were quick to defend their own athletes against similar accusations.

How was it, Dutch journalists wanted to know, that doubts were raised about the gold-medal performances in Sydney of Peter van den Hoogenband and Inge de Bruijn, while Misty Hyman, who improved her personal best by four seconds and won a gold medal, and Dara Torres, who was out of the sport for seven years and returned to win a gold and three bronzes, were American heroes? It was, wrote Sam Donnellon in the *Philadelphia Daily News,* a good question.

Further enraging members of the IOC were American-led efforts to clean up the scandal-ridden process by which cities were chosen to host the Olympics. Amid humiliating worldwide scrutiny during the past year, several IOC members had been forced to resign for accepting expensive gifts and favors, and a trial of two top organizing officials in Salt Lake City, which would host the 2002 Winter Games, was threatening to reveal more greedy behavior and embarrass the Olympic movement further. Harassed and challenged on every side, the IOC seemed to be having a nervous breakdown at precisely the time it was standing on the world's center stage.

In the final week of competition, the Games developed an almost schizophrenic personality. As Cathy Freeman's victory in the 400 meters was reducing Australia to tears, as Michael Johnson and Maurice Greene were winning gold medals in the men's 400 and 100 respectively, as Haile Gebrselassie of Ethiopia was winning his second Olympic title at 10,000 meters, as great athletes were performing amazing feats in every venue, the unelected, unaccountable, self-perpetuating officials who run the Olympics turned the focus over to drugs.

Prince Alexandre de Merode, the chairman of the IOC medical commission, leveled the astonishing charge that five U.S. Olympic athletes had tested positive before the Seoul Olympics in 1988. He could not remember their names, he said, but he believed there had been a cover-up. Former USOC drug chief Bob Voy denied it.

American reporters responded by recalling that one of the Games' most honored champions, Heike Drechsler, was a product of East Germany's drug-saturated sports machine that won gold medals at the cost of the health of many of the country's athletes. When Heike said that two authors who wrote she had regularly been given steroids were liars, she was sued for slander, convicted of perjury, and forced to apologize. Yet here she was, back in the Olympics at the age of thirty-five.

As for nandrolone, the drug C.J. was accused of using, the cat was now out of the bag and clawing everything in sight. Merlene Ottey, who finished fourth in the 100 in Sydney, had been banned from the 1999 World Championships for using nandrolone and then reinstated. Susanthika Jayasinghe of Sri Lanka, who would win the bronze medal at 200 meters, had twice been suspended after testing positive for the drug and then allowed to return despite misgivings by the IAAF.

And yet, according to press reports, six athletes *were* kicked out of the 2000 Olympics for using nandrolone, including a Latvian rower who said he had used a Chinese herbal medicine. The IOC seemed to be having quite enough trouble dealing with a drug being used right under its nose without worrying about an athlete sitting on the sidelines.

As MARION AND C.J. met with Charlie Wells to decide what to do next, they quickly came to one conclusion. As much as possible, Marion should be kept out of it. She needed to concentrate on the job at hand, which was to try to win four more events, and nothing else. So Marion didn't read the papers, didn't log on to the Internet, watched as little television as possible, and let C.J. take charge. Fortunately, the two contacts she still had with the outside world—the telephone and e-mail—were a great source of comfort when she needed it most.

"The only thing I was getting was support, people who said it was all a bunch of BS," she said of messages that poured in from back home. "It was nice to see that every time I turned on the computer. I just put myself in a cocoon and tried to stay as focused as possible. It was good to have friends there with me."

As C.J. met with Charlie, Nike publicist Dave Mingey, and Lewis Kay, a young public relations man from Los Angeles who had been working with them during the year, two things soon became clear. The first was that they should call a press conference to answer the charges. The second was that they were alone.

There were no offers of help from the U.S. Olympic Committee, Charlie noted, no words of support or concern from USA Track & Field. Except for an old friend who was a member of the USOC, no one even called to ask how they were holding up. It was, Charlie said, an interesting way to learn who their friends were.

On Tuesday, September 26, the day of the press conference, Marion was sleeping in when C.J. came into the bedroom and said there was an old friend waiting to see her. But she wasn't up yet, Marion protested. She hadn't showered. She looked a mess. This was no time for her to be meeting people. Just go out there, C.J. said, and Marion threw on some sweat clothes, opened the door, and, smiling for the first time in two days, gave Johnnie Cochran a hug.

True to his words of more than a year earlier, Cochran, one of Marion's biggest fans since helping overturn her suspension for missing a drug test in high school, had come to Australia to see her run. Of course, he would attend the press conference as a gesture of support, he told her. Later, as Cochran watched from the wings, Charlie had to smile. Look at everybody wondering what he's doing here, he thought. Maybe we're not so alone after all.

It was decided early on that Marion should make an appearance at the press conference. Her absence might send the wrong message, and besides, she wanted everyone to know that she was firmly in C.J.'s corner. But everyone agreed that after making a brief statement she should leave. For one thing, reporters would want to question her and that would interfere with getting C.J.'s message out. And for another, she was not sure she would be able to control herself.

"It would have been difficult keeping my emotions together," she said of the prospect of watching C.J. defend himself. "I wanted to be strong, in control of the situation, and I was afraid that if I had stayed, whoever was doing this to us might have gotten what they wanted, which was to upset me. I didn't want that to happen."

She was there to show her complete support for her husband, she told the crowded news conference, which was arranged with the help of a local public relations agency at a hotel in downtown Sydney. She had complete belief that the legal system would clear his name. Then she gave C.J. a kiss and, accompanied by her security detail, went back to the apartment.

"I never thought I'd see the day you guys wanted to photograph me more than my wife," C.J. said as dozens of photographers fired off shot after shot. But soon, the jokes were gone and he broke into tears.

"I might not be the most agreeable person and I might be downright mean at times," he said, stopping occasionally to wipe his eyes and catch his breath. "But nobody on the planet can say that I don't love my wife and I don't love my kids."

After ten years of competing at the highest level of his sport, C.J. said, he was tired. He had already told Gene Cherry, a reporter in Raleigh, he would retire after the Olympics. Was it reasonable to think he would risk everything he and Marion had worked for now?

"For what?" he asked emotionally? "To win in Oslo? There is nothing I could gain from taking that risk. There's nothing. Nothing. There's nothing that I need. There's nothing that I want. There's nothing that I could gain." And he paused again to regain his composure as best he could.

He would defend himself vigorously, C.J. said. He would go through the proper channels and be exonerated. When all was said and done, the opinion people had of him would be different from what it was today.

C.J.'s defense was simple: He had not taken nandrolone pills or injected it; he had inadvertently ingested it in a food supplement. This was what had happened to Chicago Bears quarterback Jim

Miller, who tested positive for nandrolone during the 1999 National Football League season. Miller said he had failed to read the label on an over-the-counter food supplement and no league or team official ever challenged his account. Miller was suspended for four games and then rejoined the team.

Victor Conte, a nutritionist from San Francisco who was working with a number of Olympians in Sydney, told the press conference that "the data that we do have at this point strongly indicates that C. J. Hunter was not using the anabolic steroid nandrolone."

Rather, Conte said, he had been taking a legal iron supplement available at any health-food store. The problem was that some manufacturers don't clean their machines properly when switching from one supplement to another, which can cause contamination. The supplement C.J. had used, Conte noted, was the same one taken by Merlene Ottey, who had been reinstated, and former world sprint champion Linford Christie of Britain, whose suspension a few years earlier had also been overturned before, maddeningly, being imposed once again by the IAAF.

As to charges that C.J.'s drug test had revealed a level of nandrolone a thousand times over the legal limit, Conte said it wasn't true. In fact, he said, the levels "would be considered to be trace levels" and "there is no way that taking this amount of nandrolone . . . would have any performance-enhancing effect."

As the controversy raged in the days that followed, C.J. was excoriated by the IOC—Pound and Rogge, their remarks dripping with sarcasm, took particular delight in staying on the attack—and Marion could sense her entire attitude about drugs and drug testing changing.

"Before this happened, I was the first to say if you test positive you've got to pay the consequences," she said ruefully. "Now I wish I'd never said it because I'm living through it. I know my husband never did anything wrong and you have to listen to Merlene and Linford and all those other athletes who have said the same thing. It leads you to question everything."

While trying to stay calm and focused on her event, Marion knew she had caught one big break. She didn't have to compete while the emotional frenzy was at its height. The schedule didn't call for her to return to the track for three days after competing in the 100. What if she had had to go straight from the press conference to the track? she wondered. She was lucky she had been able to make her brief appearance at C.J.'s side and disappear for a few days.

Then, too, there was the fact that despite all the distractions and confusion, there was one solid rock she could lean on for support: her coach. She had worked too hard to let somebody take satisfaction from hurting her, Trevor told her. "Let's go out there and get the job done and then we'll get this taken care of," he said.

"He was just incredible," Marion said later. "He convinced me we weren't going to let anything pull us down."

From the moment the Olympic track-and-field schedule was released a year earlier, Marion knew that Wednesday, September 27, would be her hell day. She would have to compete in two rounds of the 200 and, barely an hour after the second heat, attempt to qualify for the long jump. And now, piled on top of the physical challenge, was the emotional burden as well as the public curiosity about how she would respond.

At the practice track that morning, Marion felt a little odd. She was used to other athletes staring at her, but things seemed different now. They weren't looking at her because of who she was, but because of what had happened. Or maybe she was just imagining it. She shook it off and continued warming up.

Once inside the stadium, Marion was gratified when the crowd cheered as her name was called, and she waved and smiled before settling into the blocks. How wonderful these Australian fans are, she thought. She was back where she was in control now, back where no one could hurt her.

The gun went off for the first heat of the 200, and within seconds she proved to everyone else what she already knew: She was fine. She had shut out distractions many times in the past and she would do so again. She had already won one Olympic gold medal. Now it was time to go after another one, and then the one after that.

Marion took a huge lead before the turn, then loafed home in 22.75. She was trying to give her legs a little rest, she told reporters. What was she going to do now? one of them asked. Get off them, Marion replied with a laugh.

Later that evening, Marion finished second in her second-round heat of the 200 when Melinda Gainsford-Taylor thrilled the fans by slipping in front at the wire in 22.49. But although an Australian television broadcaster tried to read something significant into the result ("Oh, Lord, what did I do?" Marion said, laughing as she watched the replay and accompanying breathless commentary that evening), no one was fooled, least of all Melinda.

"That was good fun," the Australian runner said. "Marion was slowing down and I thought, 'What the hell, I might as well win in my hometown.' They gave me a photo of the finish and I'll take it home and frame it and tell my kids twenty years from now that Mommy ran against her and helped push her."

Indeed, Marion was running so smoothly and effortlessly that the final of the 200 on Thursday was now a foregone conclusion. Her second gold medal was a lock.

An hour later, Marion finished the draining day with a flourish, qualifying for the long jump on her first attempt with a leap of 22-3. Only Heike Drechsler and Fiona May had better jumps, and just slightly better ones at that.

"Woo," Marion shouted as she ran up to a television camera and waved, "we can go home for the night."

First, though, she had one more thing to do before her return from the nightmare of the past few days would be complete. She had to walk off the track and look a curious world straight in the eye.

During the next hour, Marion talked to Jim Gray of NBC and to an interviewer for the French television network. She talked to Spanish television and to broadcasters from Sweden, Mexico, Australia, and the BBC. Some radio correspondents gathered around, and more from television, and then, in the mixed zone underneath the stands, a crowd of print reporters ten rows deep.

"This is where I love to be," Marion said. "In front of the fans, under the lights. It kind of gets my mind off everything. When I stood on the track this morning all the things that have happened over the last couple of days pushed to the back of my mind. It's all about business now."

It was important to do this, Marion said later. She hadn't let the events of the past few days affect the way she trained or ran, had she? Why should she let them affect the way she dealt with reporters? They had their job to do and she was part of it. Besides, the media had respected her request that she not be hounded with questions she couldn't answer about events beyond her control. It was only right that she respect them now.

Marion's return to the Olympic Stadium was the subject of intense scrutiny by hundreds of journalists, and more than a few came away thinking her response after competing might have been at least as impressive as her accomplishments on the track.

"Through all the controversy swirling around her," wrote Tom Powers in the *St. Paul Pioneer Press,* "Marion Jones handled herself with remarkable grace and dignity."

"There is only one thing you can be absolutely certain of around here, and it says more about Jones than any medal total she could possibly attain," wrote Mark Kreidler in the *Sacramento Bee.* "Whatever happens in Sydney, it will not be because Marion Jones couldn't handle the pressure."

ON THURSDAY, MARION won the gold medal in the 200-meter dash in 21.84 seconds, the fastest time in the world to date and .43 seconds ahead of Pauline Davis-Thompson of the Bahamas. Though all eight finalists ran their best times of the year, it was the largest margin of victory in the 200 since Wilma Rudolph won by .45 seconds at the Tokyo Olympics in 1960.

"My best test will be tomorrow," Marion said of the upcoming final in the long jump. "I hope none of you doubted me in the sprints."

HEIKE DRECHSLER'S EYES were closed. Her third jump of the evening, 22-11¼, had given her the lead in the finals of the long-jump competition and she had one jump remaining. So did Marion.

There was no doubt this time that Marion would survive the

cut and be around for her final three jumps. Unlike the agony of Sacramento, where her first two jumps were foul, she had gotten off two good efforts in the early going and the best of them, 22-8¼, had put her in third place behind Heike and Fiona May. But Marion fouled on her next two jumps, which didn't appear long enough to take the lead in any case, and now she was down to one last chance to keep her gold medal streak alive.

Marion had felt fast and loose on the runway the entire evening. The night was surprisingly hot, the wind relatively gentle, and she could feel the spring in her legs. She was flying down the runway, she thought. The big jump she needed was very much within reach. All she had to do was let it rip.

Concentrating as she stood at the head of the runway, Marion could hardly keep from smiling. This is what every athlete dreams about, isn't it? The last shot in the NBA Finals. The last play in the Super Bowl. The last jump in the Olympics. Go for it, she told herself. Don't hold back. It's yours for the taking. Take it.

She bounced up and down, bent over, swung her arms back and forth once, twice, three times. She stood up, looked down the runway, blew out a deep breath, and she was off. Heike closed her eyes.

The moment Marion landed two things were immediately clear. The first was that the jump was a winner—well past twenty-three feet, closer to twenty-four perhaps—and by far the longest jump anywhere in the world all year. The second was that the jump was foul. She had been over the board by several inches. She had finished third.

"If you could put into words how I felt at that moment it would be Ooooooo," Marion said later, letting out a sigh of disappointment, relief, and a little pain. "I looked around and saw the man flip up the red flag. All my hopes were dashed."

Thrilled to have won her second Olympic long jump title eight years after the first, Heike couldn't resist celebrating with one last superfluous jump. She stood at the head of the runway, clapped her hands rhythmically over her head to liven up the crowd, and did a little shimmy with her hips. Sitting on a bench nearby, Marion joined in the fun, clapping and laughing, too, as Heike ran through the sand.

Later, in the interview room, the women traded extravagant compliments.

"Marion is a great fighter," Heike said. "She has so much speed on the runway. If she can only get that run-up right, she can be truly great. She is the future."

"You have to applaud Heike," Marion said. "I can tell my grandkids in thirty years I competed against one of the best long jumpers ever."

Someone asked Marion if she had any regrets, which brought groans from a number of reporters. It was, wrote Steve Wilstein of the Associated Press, the silliest question anyone ever asked her. Of course, she could have avoided the risk to her body and her reputation by not competing in the long jump, Wilstein wrote. But that's not the way she thinks, and it's not the way champions act.

"If life teaches us anything," wrote Mike Celizik in New Jersey's *Bergen Record*, "it is that great achievements are not possible without great dreams. The crime is not in failing to reach your dreams, but in not having them."

THE U.S. WOMEN'S RELAY picture was a mess. Inger Miller, whose injury had forced her to miss the 200, was officially out of the 4×100, too, which meant she would not compete in the Olympics at all, and Gail Devers had joined her on the sidelines. In the first heat of the 100-meter hurdles Wednesday night, Devers, who had won the 100 in the previous two Olympics, aggravated a hamstring injury she suffered in Brussels in August.

Suddenly, two of the top sprinters in the U.S. were out of the race, and since Marion was the only American to make the 100-meter final, it was far from clear the team had enough depth to make up for their loss. But as Marion competed in the long jump Friday, the U.S. runners were heartened when they were barely nosed out in the relay semifinals by a strong team from the Bahamas that had won the World Championship in Seville in 1999.

"It's good to know we've got it going on our own," Nanceen Perry told reporters. "With Marion in there, we'll do even better."

"Marion is the missile," said U.S. coach Karen Dennis. "She'll bring it in."

The 4×400 was also worrisome. None of the three U.S. runners had gotten as far as the semifinals of the open 400, which Cathy Freeman had won before her adoring Australian fans. Michelle Collins, Marion's friend and teammate, was out with a stress fracture, and her spot would go to Monique Hennagan.

And just to make the challenge even more difficult, the two relays would be run almost back-to-back, at 7:40 P.M. and 9:35 P.M. on Saturday. After running in eight races, after competing twice in the long jump, after living through an emotional upheaval in the glare of a worldwide spotlight, Marion would finish the Olympics running two relay legs in less than two hours.

"NANCEEN! SLOW DOWN!" Torri Edwards yelled at Nanceen Perry as she completed the second leg of the 4×100 close to the lead. Nanceen stopped accelerating and then heard the yell again. "Slow down!" By the time the abortive pass was complete, the teams from the Bahamas and Jamaica were well ahead and the chances that the U.S. would win a relay it hadn't lost since the boycotted Moscow Games of 1980 were not good. They soon got worse.

Nanceen's pass to Marion also took too long to complete, and when she was finally off she was too far behind Debbie Ferguson of the Bahamas to catch up. Running as hard as she could, Marion nosed out Christine Arron for the bronze medal.

"I was running scared," Debbie said. "I knew Marion was coming."

Nanceen said she wished there had been more time to practice the exchanges, but Marion didn't accept that as an excuse. The U.S. had had a number of training sessions, she said, although perhaps not quite as many as the Bahamas.

"We had a chance," she said after congratulating Chandra Sturrup, who had helped give the Bahamas their only gold medal of the Games. "There was just too much ground to make up."

Hurrying back to the warm-up area to discuss tactics for the 4×400, Marion felt depressed, nervous, and suddenly very tired. Perhaps it would be best, she told Karen Dennis, if she didn't run the anchor. She couldn't be sure how her legs would feel coming around the final turn. She didn't know how much she had left. "Let me run third," Marion said. "I think I can give you a good third leg." Dennis agreed and named Latasha Colander-Richardson to run the anchor leg.

Marion sat with Trevor before she returned to the track for one last pep talk. He was so proud of her, he said. One more race and they could all go home. He wanted her to run those last 100 meters like she had never run them before.

"I'll do my best," Marion said, "but make sure you have an ambulance and a stretcher at the finish line."

"I can't promise you that," he said, "but I'll be there for you with open arms."

Back at the track, Marion's spirits were suddenly lifted by the sight of her teammates gathered at the start line. They were waiting for her, counting on her. She had a job to do. Just the thought of it made her feel better.

Running the first leg, Jearl Miles-Clark, a thirty-four-year-old veteran running in her third Olympics, summoned up a big kick coming around the final turn and handed Monique Hennagan the lead. Monique finished her lap about even with Catherine Scott of Jamaica, and Marion, urging her on with waves of her hand, took the baton about the same time as Deon Hemmings began Jamaica's third leg. The race was on.

Marion felt relaxed as she ran down the opening straightaway and she glanced up at the big video screen above the stands to see where she stood in relation to the other teams. Then, as she came off the first turn, it hit her. She felt good. She felt surprisingly good. She felt better, in fact, than she had ever felt running the 400 before. She started running faster.

Oops, Deon thought as Marion's lead increased. "If I went out that fast I would die at the end," she said later. "That's embarrassing."

Oh, my God, she keeps getting farther and farther ahead, thought Melinda Gainsford-Taylor, who was running the third leg for Australia and realized she would soon have another story to tell her children in twenty years. "That was a bit awful. I thought she might get tired, but no way."

Asked for her impression of Marion, Allison Curbishly of Britain said, "All I saw was the back of her head."

By the time she came out of the final turn, Marion's lead was up to five meters, and as she hit the straightaway Trevor's words came back to her—run the last 100 meters like she'd never run them before. As she picked up the pace, increasing her lead with every step, she wondered if she was overdoing it.

"I was concerned my legs were going to say, 'No more, Marion, no more,'" she said later. "But they didn't."

When Marion handed the baton to Latasha, she led by fifteen meters, a huge margin, and the crowd was screaming. Though Jamaica's Lorraine Graham made a late charge on the final leg, the U.S. won by more than half a second, in 3:22.62. Marion's leg, 49.40, equaled that of Cathy Freeman on the fifth-place Australian team, and, although the clocking was unofficial, was second in the world all year only to the 49.11 Freeman had run to win the gold medal a few days earlier.

"That was one of the smoothest legs in the 400 that I've ever seen," Jearl Miles-Clark said later. "I'm just glad she was on my team."

"Thank God she lit the burners," said Monique.

"When you take on such a task, it's almost hard to believe," said Pauline Davis-Thompson, who had run on the Bahamian team that won the 4×100. "Much respect for Marion Jones. I say, 'You go, girl.'"

Marion hugged Latasha, Jearl hugged Monique, they all hugged each other and mugged for the photographers. Then, almost involuntarily, with a sigh as big as her smile, Marion looked straight into a camera and said, "We're done. We're done."

With five medals in five different events, Marion became the most decorated track-and-field athlete, male or female, ever to emerge from a single Olympics. If she felt any frustration, it was not because two of her medals were bronze but because they had almost been gold.

"They were all right there," Marion said of losing the long jump by three inches and the 4×100 because of two injuries and two faulty baton passes. "Even people who doubted me have to question their doubt now because it was right there. But overall I'm very satisfied. And I'm looking forward to Athens. I've already won some big races there, you know."

IN THE DAYS AND WEEKS AFTER the Olympics, Marion received thousands of e-mail messages from dozens of countries all over the world. Many expressed their admiration for her accomplishments, her spirit, and her grace under the pressure of the events swirling around her. Others wrote to say she had convinced them to take up running, or to work hard at other pursuits. Still more offered congratulations on her twenty-fifth birthday, which she celebrated on October 12.

A number of the e-mails were in languages the correspondents surely knew Marion could not read, but sent anyway. They just wanted to make contact, they seemed to be saying. They wanted Marion to know they were thinking of her even if she could not understand their exact words.

One message spoke directly to her goal of trying to win five gold medals. Marion should not be disappointed, the writer said. She had reached for the stars and hit the moon.

## ACKNOWLEDGMENTS

*T*his book owes a great debt to Duncan Murrell, a young editor who was intrigued by what Marion and I were up to and who became our chief advocate at Algonquin Books. In the months that followed, Duncan offered a steady stream of support, ideas, and assistance, all of which were much appreciated. Shannon Ravenel and Elisabeth Scharlatt of Algonquin were also among our early supporters, as was my agent, Mike Hamilburg, and his associate, Joan Socola. I am grateful to them all, as well as to Charles F. Harris, the editorial director of Amistad Press, and Sarah Wharton, for overseeing this updated paperback version of the book.

It does not seem necessary to mention again the names of all the people who have crossed Marion's path over the years and are quoted in these pages. It does seem necessary, however, to thank them once more for offering a stranger so much of their time and patience and so many of their memories. I was gratified by how eager most of them were to talk to me, and startled when, after word of the project began to get around, I began hearing from people demanding they be allowed to tell me *their* favorite stories about Marion. After a while, I had a joke with Marion that one day I would pick up the phone or knock at a door and be told, "Who? Marion Jones? Sorry, can't say she made much of an impression." It never happened. Not even close.

The more time I spent around Marion's support group, the more I began to think of her as a track-and-field version of Billie Holiday, whose imperishable recordings I believe are due in part to the fact she never let a mediocre musician anywhere near her. Marion's sidemen seem equally remarkable to me and I think they share the credit for her success.

Trevor Graham is simply one of the finest men I have ever known in the coaching profession. His knowledge, intelligence, and coolness under fire are unsurpassed in my experience, and I am grateful for the time he spent explaining the intricacies of his work with Marion, and for his many other kindnesses, and those of his wife, Ann, as well.

Charlie Wells and his assistants at Vector Sports Management, Paulette Chandler and Anna Bedell, were indispensable in keeping me up-to-date on Marion's schedule, providing background information, and helping with travel arrangements. Their greatest coup was helping me secure a pass at the World Championships in Seville that allowed access to the athletes' training area as well as the press center. Rather than saying MEDIA, it read PERSONAL COACH. Best pass I've ever had, believe me.

Thanks to Marion's medical team—doctors Steve Bernabeu and Norman Levin, and massage therapists Marvin Finger and Chris Whetstine—who were unfailingly helpful in describing the ups and downs of Marion's physical condition, and who were great company as well. I am also indebted to Chris for sharing his e-mail message describing Marion's visit to the clinic in Soweto.

Thanks to Marion's teammates—Antonio Pettigrew, Chandra Sturrup, Jerome Young, Michelle Collins, and Brian Frasure—whom I greatly enjoyed getting to know and whose professionalism and dedication I came to admire.

Thanks to Dana Gelin and Dave Lohse of the University of North Carolina sports information department for opening their files, answering dozens of questions, and providing so many of the photographs. At USA Track & Field, thanks to Tom Surber, Hal Bateman, Jennifer Tilden, and Glen McMicken of the communications department. Thanks to Dave Mingey at Nike and Lewis Kay. And a special thank-you to Peter Larsson, who runs an astonishing track-and-field Web site and has the answers to even the most arcane questions at his fingertips.

Thanks to Bill Adee, the sports editor of the *Chicago Sun-Times*, for allowing me to disappear at various times these last two years, and for pretending not to notice when more track-and-field items than usual made their way into my "Between the Lines" column for the *Sun-Times*.

Thanks to journalists Philip Hersh, Randy Harvey, Maryann Hudson, Tim Layden, John Ortega, David Kirvin, Eric Sondheimer, Lisa O'Donnell, Neil Amato, Woody Woodburn, Alan Abrahamson, Nick Paumgarten, David Evans, John Mehaffey, Anthony Jeffries, Garry Hill, Sieg Lindstrom, Robbi Pickeral, Scott Lacy, Kennedy Cosgrove, Stephen Wilson, Gene Cherry, Bert Rosenthal, Louise Evans, Ned Barnett, Amy Shipley, Jemele Hill, Mike Penner, Jere Longman, Don Bosley, J. Freedom du Lac, Aileen Voisin, Jo-Ann Barnas, Barbara Heubner, Rob Gloster, Bob Baum, Stephen Wilson, and Rakesh Rao. Their work and ideas were helpful in many ways, not the least of them increasing my understanding of the occasionally opaque world of track and field. And thanks to track impresarios Al and Don Franken and the legendary Art Hoffman, whose dedication to and knowledge of the sport borders on the frightening.

Thanks to Albert Kelly for his account of his sister's younger days, to C.J. Hunter for his invaluable assistance, to Marion's longtime friends Bernadine and Janelle Simon, to Jim O'Brien at Thousand Oaks High School, and to Jean Lenti Ponsetto at De-Paul University. To Mike and Gail Downey, *That's amore,* and thanks for the use of the hall. Thanks to Marsha A. Kunin and Carol Slezak for approaching the manuscript with fresh eyes and sharp pencils, and a special thank-you to Joan and Julie Rapoport, who were once again my copy readers of last resort.

Finally I would like to thank Marion Toler for honoring her daughter's request to speak with me about many things, including some she retrieved from her memory at the cost of some painful moments she did not deserve.

"Marion," her mother said, "if I talk to Ron, I'm going to tell the truth."

"Mom," Marion replied, "that's what I want you to do."

When Marion was in high school, she told an interviewer that hers was "the mother of all mothers."

I agree.

Ron Rapoport is a sports columnist for the *Chicago Sun-Times* and sports commentator for National Public Radio's *Weekend Edition with Scott Simon*. He has written a number of collaborative books, including *Betty Garrett and Other Songs: A Life on Stage and Screen,* and is the editor of *A Kind of Grace: A Treasury of Sportswriting by Women.*